John Herbert Slater

The Romance of Book-Collecting

John Herbert Slater

The Romance of Book-Collecting

ISBN/EAN: 9783744771504

Printed in Europe, USA, Canada, Australia, Japan

Cover: Foto ©ninafisch / pixelio.de

More available books at **www.hansebooks.com**

THE ROMANCE OF BOOK-COLLECTING.

TAMERLANE

AND

OTHER POEMS.

BY A BOSTONIAN.

*Young heads are giddy, and young hearts are warm,
And make mistakes for manhood to reform.* —COWPER.

BOSTON:
CALVIN F. S. THOMAS.....PRINTER.

1827.

Fac-simile of original cover of Poe's Tamerlane.
Frontispiece. *See page* 138.

THE ROMANCE

OF

BOOK - COLLECTING.

BY

J. H. SLATER,

Editor of 'Book Prices Current;' Author of 'Early Editions,
'Round and About the Bookstalls,' 'The Library Manual,'
'Engravings and their Value,' etc., etc.

LONDON:
ELLIOT STOCK, 62, PATERNOSTER ROW, E.C.
1898.

CONTENTS.

CHAPTER.	PAGE
I. IN EULOGY OF CATALOGUES	1
II. A COMPARISON OF PRICES	15
III. SOME LUCKY FINDS	32
IV. THE FORGOTTEN LORE SOCIETY	50
V. SOME HUNTING-GROUNDS OF LONDON	73
VI. VAGARIES OF BOOK-HUNTERS	92
VII. HOW FASHION LIVES	112
VIII. THE RULES OF THE CHASE	126
IX. THE GLAMOUR OF BINDINGS	140
X. THE HAMMER AND THE END	162

CHAPTER I.

IN EULOGY OF CATALOGUES.

THERE are plenty of people—in fact, they are in the great majority even among bookish men—who regard antiquated sale-catalogues in the light of so much rubbish, and yet, when intelligently consulted, these memorials of a bygone day not only have their uses, but are positively interesting. Truly enough they are not popular, like the last new novel which, for one reason or another, has taken the town by storm, and it would not pay to reprint a single one of them, even the best or most important that has ever held the frequenters of auction-rooms spell-bound.

Sometimes a 'parcel' will be sold for what it will fetch, and on investigation may prove to contain a few simple-minded pamphlets on subjects of no importance, 'and others,' the latter consisting of book-catalogues of the last or the earlier portion of the present century. This happens sufficiently often to make it possible for a bookish enthusiast of an antiquarian turn of mind to lose himself with marvellous rapidity in a maze of old-time dispersions. But the enthusiast, unless very determined indeed, knows better than to choke his library with such material. He is aware that an exhaustive index is indispensable to the proper appreciation of such literature, and to make that would occupy his nights indefinitely.

And so it comes to pass that old sale-catalogues of books are consigned for the most part to the rubbish-heap, or perhaps sent to the mills, to reappear later on in another guise. They may be scarce in the sense that, if you wanted a particular one, it could only be got with great difficulty, and at considerable expense (here the art of selling to advantage comes in), or perhaps not at all. This, however, makes no matter, for the fact remains that such things are not inquired for as a general rule, and that an occasional demand is insufficient to give them any kind of a status in the world of letters.

Some five or six years ago a member of the Johnson Club, a literary society which meets at intervals in various parts of London, but more particularly in Fleet Street, discovered a catalogue of the sale of the old Doctor's library, neatly marked with the prices each book had brought. Whether this was a sale *post mortem* or a casual interlocutory dispersal at the instance of some soulless creditor, I do not know. In any case the relic was a find—a fact which the bookseller who bought it was not slow to appreciate, for he at once assessed its value, to the society man, at something like forty shillings. This was paid without demur, because at the time all the other Johnson catalogues were in mufti, and it had struck no one to exhibit them, and also because it was, under the circumstances of the case, a very desirable memorial to present to the society which flourishes on the fame of the great lexicographer. Here, at any rate, is one exceptional instance of an old catalogue possessing a distinct pecuniary value up to £2, and though the noise this discovery made in certain circles led to a general search and the rescue of other copies, the circumstances are not in the least affected on that account.

From a literary or even a sentimental standpoint, a long story, full of speculation and romance, might be written on Dr. Johnson's long-forgotten catalogue. We might, for instance, trace, by the aid of Boswell, many of the books mentioned in it to the very hand of the master himself. We might conjecture the use he made of this volume or that in his 'Lives of the Poets,' 'The Vanity of Human Wishes,' or in the ponderous Dictionary that cemented his fame, and by way of interlude beguile an hour occasionally by contrasting the character of the books he affected with the quality of those on the shelves of some modern Johnson, assuming, of course, that his counterpart is to be found. Then we might look at the prices realized, and compare them with those ruling at the present day. Some books then in fashion are, we may be sure, now despised and rejected, others have not been appreciably affected by the course of time, while others, again, are now sought after throughout the world, and are hardly to be met with at all. There is no old catalogue whatever which is not capable of affording considerable instruction if we only read between the lines.

Then, again, there is one speculation that no true book-lover can stifle; it haunts him as he passes the barrows with their loads of sermons and scholastic primers, and it is this: 'Time works wonders.' Some day may not this heterogeneous mass of rubbish produce as fine a pearl as ever a diseased oyster was robbed of? May not fashion go off at a tangent, and dote on lexicons or what not? There have been men— Rossi, for example, who was so saturated with the suspicion that fashion might change any moment that the stalls by which he passed were 'like towns through which Attila or the Tartars had swept, with ruin in their train'—who would buy any book whatever, whether they wanted it or not, on the bare chance of someone else wanting it, either at the time or in the days to come.

Such may be the outcome of a too eager perusal of catalogues, focussed till it produces an absorbing passion, which only departs with life itself. After a time discrimination, naturally enough, becomes impossible, and whole masses of books are bought

In Eulogy of Catalogues

up for what they may become, not for what they are. This may appear to be an ignoble sort of pastime, but in reality it is far otherwise, since wholesale purchasers of this stamp are invariably well read, and know more about their author than his mere name. I personally was acquainted with a bookworm who absorbed whole collections at a time. His house was full of books; they were under the beds, in cupboards, piled up along the walls, under the tables and chairs, and even on the rafters under the roof. If you walked without due care, you would, more likely than not, tumble over a folio in the dark, or bring down a wall of literature, good, bad, or indifferent, on your head. This library was chaotic to the general, though the worm himself knew very well where to burrow for anything he required, and, what is more to the point, would feed for hours on volumes that few people had ever so much as heard of. The monetary value of his treasures did not trouble him, though one of his favourite anecdotes related to the hunting down of a fourth folio Shakespeare, which, after much haggling, he purchased for a song from a poor woman who lived in an almshouse. When the delight of the chase was over, he recompensed her to the full market value, thereby proving that, in his case at least, a greed for books does not necessarily carry with it a stifled conscience. Sad to relate, this bibliophile died like other men, and the collection of a lifetime came to the inevitable hammer. Most of his books then proved to be portions of sets. If a work were complete in, say, ten volumes, he would perhaps possess no more than five or six of the full number in various bindings and editions, while others, though complete, were imperfect, and many were in rags. Yet among the whole there were some pearls of great price. Even in his day the fashion had changed in his favour.

Now, this changing of fashion which is always going on cannot be prophesied at haphazard, or perhaps even at all; but if there is a way of forestalling it, it is by the careful comparison of prices realized for books of a certain kind at different periods of time, and this can only be accomplished by a study of catalogues. The book-man likes to think that history repeats itself in this as in other matters, and that what has happened once will probably occur again in process of time. Nay, he might, without any great stretch of credulity, persuade himself that it *must* occur, if only he live long enough. That's the rub, for half a dozen lifetimes might not be sufficient to witness a return to favour of, say, the ponderous works of the Fathers, which were in such great demand a couple of centuries ago. As of them, so of many other kinds of books which are only read now by the very few. Some day they will rise again after their long sleep, but not for us.

As a corollary to this eulogy of catalogues, let us take a few of them and see where the book-man's steps are leading him. In his wanderings abroad he must many a time be painfully conscious of the fact that his own quest is that of everyone else whose tastes are similar to his own. Let a first edition of the immortal 'Angler' so much as peep from among the grease and filth of a rag-and-bone shop, and a magnetic current travels at lightning speed to the homes of a score or more of pickers-up of unconsidered trifles, who forthwith race for the prize. How they get to know of its existence is a mystery. Perhaps some strange psychological influence is at work to prompt them to dive down a pestilential alley for the first and last time in their lives. Did you ever see a millionaire groping in the gutter for a dropped coin? His energy is nothing to that of the book-man who has reason to suspect—why he knows not—that here or there may perhaps lie hid and unrecognised a volume which fashion has made omnipotent. And his energy is not confined to himself alone, for one decree of a naughty world changes not—it is ever the same: What many men want, more men will search for; what one man only has, many will want. The path of the book-hunter is trodden flat and hard with countless footsteps, and this is the reason why it is so unsatisfactory to look specially for anything valuable.

We may take it, therefore, that, though hunting for books may be a highly exhilarating pastime, it is seldom remunerative from a pecuniary point of view. There are, no doubt, hundreds of thousands of good and useful volumes which can be bought at any time for next to nothing; but they have no halo round them at the moment, and so they are abandoned to their fate by the typical collector, who insists not only on having the best editions in exchange for his money, but that his books shall be of a certain description—that is to say, of a kind to please him, or which for the time being is in great demand.

And men are pleased at various times by books of a widely different character, as the old catalogues tell us plainly enough. In 1676, when William Cooper, bookseller, dwelling at the Sign of the Pelican in Little Britain, held the first auction sale ever advertised in England—that of the library of Dr. Lazarus Seaman—works of the Fathers and Schoolmen; learned and critical volumes of distressing profundity, appealed to the comparative few who could read and write sufficiently well to make reading a pleasurable occupation. Poetry is absent entirely. Shakespeare and Milton are elbowed out by Puritan fanatics who fulminate curses against mankind. No doubt, if a book-man of those days had been asked what kind of literature would be in vogue a couple of centuries hence, he would have pointed to Seaman's collection and replied, 'Books like those can never die. So long as learning holds its sway over the few, they will be bought and treasured by the many.' In this he would have been wrong, for few people

In Eulogy of Catalogues 9

care nowadays for volumes such as these. The times have changed utterly, and we with them.

At this same sale was a book which sold for less than almost any other, and it lay hidden away under this bald and misleading title: 'Veteris et Novi Testamenti in Ling. Indica, Cantabr. in Nova Anglia.' Simply this, and nothing more. No statement as to date, condition or binding appears in Cooper's catalogue, and yet this Bible is none other than John Eliot's translation into the Indian language, with a metrical version of the Psalms in the same vernacular, published at Cambridge, Mass., in 1663-61. An auctioneer of the present day would print the title of this volume in large capitals, and tell us whether or no it had the rare dedication to King Charles II., of pious memory, which was only inserted in twenty copies sent to England as presents. If it had, then this book, wherever it may be, is now worth much more than its weight in gold, for at Lord Hardwicke's sale, held in London on June 29, 1888, such a desirable copy was knocked down for £580.

Why this immense advance in price, seeing that probably there is no man in England to-day who could read a single line of John Eliot's free translation? The reason is plain. Since 1661 sleepy New England has vanished like the light canoes of countless Indians, and in the busy United States there has grown up a great demand for anything which illustrates the early history of

North America. Had such a contingency struck old Lazarus Seaman, he would have made his will to suit the exigences of the case, and perhaps taken more interest in John Eliot and his missionary enterprises than anyone did at the time, or has done since.

It may perhaps be said that Seaman's library must have been of a special kind, one which such a learned divine might be expected to gather within his walls; but as a matter of fact this was not so. Between 1676 and 1682, October to October in each of those years, exactly thirty sales of books were held by auction in London, among them the libraries of Sir Kenelm Digby, Dr. Castell, the author of the 'Lexicon Heptaglotton,' Dr. Gataker, Lord Warwick, and other noted persons. The general character of all the seventeenth-century catalogues which time has spared for our perusal is substantially the same. Every one of them reflects the taste and fashion of the day, as did Agrippa's magic glass the forms of absent friends. Still harping chiefly on theology! as Polonius might say, these catalogues are crammed with polemics and books of grave discourse. Anything which could not, by hook or by crook, be dragged, as to its contents, within the circumference of the fashionable craze, was disposed of for a trifling sum. Even in 1682 the learned world, or at least our narrow corner of it, was inhabited almost entirely by crop-eared Puritans, with sugar-loaf hats on their

In Eulogy of Catalogues 11

heads and broad buckles to their shoes, and by Philosophers. True! Cromwell had gone to his account, and Charles II. held Court at St. James's and elsewhere, but the King and his merry companions were not reading men—unless a profound knowledge of 'Hudibras,' that book which Pepys could not abide the sight of, could make them so. The anti-Puritans patronized Butler, and doted on Sir Charles Sedley, the Earl of Rochester and a few more, who scribbled love-verses by day, and gambled and fought and drank at night. But these worshipped Thalia and Erato only, with music and dancing and other delights, and knew nothing of solid hard work by the midnight oil. They had no books to speak of, and the few they had were light and airy like themselves, and for the most part as worthless.

On November 25, 1678, a great sale was held at the White Hart, in Bartholomew Close. The books were 'bought out of the best libraries abroad, and out of the most eminent seats of learning beyond the seas,' or, more truthfully, had been removed from the shops of seven London book-sellers who had combined to 'rig' the market. Books of all kinds were dispersed at this sale, which continued *de die in diem* till the heptarchy was satisfied. Were the members of this pioneer combination alive now, they would weep to think that they gave away on that occasion — practically gave away — scores of what have long since become aristocrats among books. Americana were there in plenty, and some of these are now so extremely rare and valuable that they are hardly to be procured for love or money; some few, indeed, have completely disappeared, tossed lightly aside, probably by disgusted purchasers, or carted back again to the shops from whence they came, to be stacked once more till they perished utterly of damp and neglect, moth, mice and rust.

On the other hand our old friends, the Puritans, revelled in grim folios bought up at prices which, the change in the value of money notwithstanding, would hardly be exceeded now. Walton's 'Biblia Sacra Polyglotta' was an immense favourite, a distinction it doubtless deserved, and, indeed, deserves yet, though we can see that Walton must have 'gone down' woefully in the last hundred years, when we come to calculate the necessaries of life that could be bought then with a piece of gold, and to contrast them with the meagre display such a sum would purchase now. The truth, perhaps, is that, although education was less widely diffused in the days of the Stuarts, it was more deep and thorough. A savant was then like a huge octopus that devastates whole districts, and daily grows fatter and more bloated at the expense of everything that moves within reach of its spreading tendrils.

To this effect are we taught by these ancient catalogues, which, however, do not exhaust all their interest in mere matters of prices and

In Eulogy of Catalogues

fashion. We can learn much from their pages and advertisements of the manners and customs of our ancestors in Bookland. It seems that there were travelling auctioneers a couple of centuries ago who prefaced their remarks with eulogies of the Mayor and Corporation of each town at which they stopped, by way, no doubt, of securing their patronage. Sales began at eight o'clock in the morning then, and went on, with a mid-day interval for refreshment, until late at night. Sometimes the auctioneer sold by the candle-end; that is to say, lit a morsel of candle on putting up some coveted volume for competition, and knocked it down to him who had bid the most when the light flickered out. This was, distinctly, an excellent method for bolstering up excitement, for every splutter must have been good for a hasty advance, regretted very possibly when the modicum of tallow entered on a fresh lease of life. When not selling by the candle-end, an auctioneer would dispose of about thirty lots in the course of an hour, and was quite willing to accept the most trifling bids. Business is more rapidly conducted now, for few auctioneers stop to curse their fate, or to regale their audience with anecdotes, as one George Smalridge, who in 1689 wrote and published a skit on the prevalent way of doing business, says was quite the usual custom in his day. His tract is written in Latin, under the title 'Auctio Davisiana,' and gives a fanciful account of the extraordinary proceedings that took place at the sale of the books of Richard Davis, an ancient bookseller of Oxford, who had fallen into the clutches of the bailiffs. The auctioneer commences with a dirge said, or perhaps sung, over the miserable Davis : ' O the vanity of human wishes ! O the changeableness of fate and its settled unkindness to us,' etc. Each book is extolled at length, and there are pages of lamentation and woe as Hobbes of Malmesbury, his ' Leviathan,' 'a very large and famous beast,' is knocked down, by mistake, for the miserable sum of five pieces of silver.

An exhaustive chapter on early book auctions would necessarily commence with the dispersion of the stock of Bonaventure and Abraham Elzevir at Leyden in April, 1653; but the Elzevirs must look to themselves, nor are these remarks intended to be even approximately full. Rather are they discursive, and in praise of catalogues in the mass; intended merely to put someone else with more space and time at his disposal in the way of rescuing them from the neglect into which they have fallen. The next chapter is more specific, for in that we will take a very famous sale of less antiquity, and endeavour to draw comparisons between then and now. And these comparisons will perhaps be very odious, for they will necessarily appeal directly to the cupidity of every bookworm that breathes, to every book-hunter who prowls around in search of rarities, and returns home—empty handed.

CHAPTER II.

A COMPARISON OF PRICES.

THE important sale to which reference was made in the last chapter is that of the library of John, Duke of Roxburghe, which was dispersed on May 18, 1812, and forty-one following days, by Robert H. Evans, a bookseller of Pall Mall. This sale is of extreme interest for two reasons. In the first place, the collection was the most extensive, varied, and important that had hitherto been offered for sale in England, or, indeed, anywhere else; and, secondly, it may fairly be regarded in the light of a connecting-link between the old state of things and the new. The Roxburghe library was not 'erected,' as Gabriel Naudæus has it, on traditional principles; it was of a general character that appealed to all classes of book-men. On the other hand, it was not quite such a library as a collector of large means might be expected to get together at the present day, for the tendency is now to specialize, and in any case many of the books that the Duke obviously took an interest in are of such little importance now, and so infrequently inquired for, that they would most assuredly be refused admission to any private library of equal importance and magnitude. Even a general lover would hardly be likely to manifest much interest in a number of volumes on Scots law or to hob-a-nob with Cheyne, who in 1720 wrote a book on the gout, or with Sir R. Blackmore, notwithstanding that eminent physician's great experience of the spleen and vapours. That lore of this kind has its merits I dispute in no way, but it is not exactly of a kind to interest the modern collector, who, even if he aim at all branches of literature alike, would much prefer to have his legal and medical instruction boiled down, so to speak, to the compass of a good digest or cyclopædia.

Nevertheless, May 18, 1812, is among the *fasti* of those who to a love of letters add a passion for books. It is the opening day of the new régime—the birthday, in fact, of those who revel in first editions and early English texts. Brunet said that the 'thermometer of bibliomania' —objectionable word!—'attained its maximum in England' during these forty-two days of ceaseless hammering, and Dibdin went perfectly insane whenever he thought of this 'Waterloo among book-battles,' as he called it. Everyone of course knows the chief episode; that struggle between Earl Spencer and the Marquis of Blandford for the 1471 Boccaccio, in its faded yellow morocco binding, and how the latter carried it off for

A Comparison of Prices 17

£2,260, a most idiotic price to pay, as subsequent events abundantly proved; for seven years later, when Lord Blandford's library came to be sold, the coveted volume was acquired by his former rival for considerably less than half the money. In now reposes in state at Manchester, or, as some choose to say, is in prison there, though it is perhaps too much to expect that all good things should be forcibly removed to London, as some greedy Metropolitans wish them to be.

The Duke of Roxburghe's library comprised rather more than 10,000 works in about 30,000 volumes, and the auctioneer's method of classifying this large assortment was so peculiar that he feels constrained to apologize for it in a rather extensive preface.

'For instance,' says he, 'the *Festyvale* of Caxton, printed in two columns, of which no other copy is at present known, may be found classed with a small edition of the Common Prayer of one shilling value.'

The 'Festyval' brought £105, and the little Prayer-Book, which proves to have been printed at London in 1707, 8s. 6d., which is more than it would be at all likely to sell for now. But what about Caxton's lordly tome; how much might that be expected to bring in case it should once again find its way into the open market? Judging from the present price of Caxtons, perhaps five or six times the money would not be an impossible figure, but there is no telling. It might bring more, even though it has the misfortune to belong to the second edition, for only six copies are known, and several of those are imperfect. Of the first edition of 1483, only three perfect copies are to be met with, and that is, of course, quite a different matter. The auctioneer need not, as it happens, have sought to excuse himself so energetically for placing good and bad books side by side, for the whole catalogue is arranged under subjects, and to do otherwise would have been manifestly impossible. He might, however, have entered somewhat more fully into detail as to condition and binding, for some of the books were, confessedly, 'thumbed to tatters,' and a suspicion that this or that 'lot' may be so afflicted lurks in every page of the catalogue.

The first book brought to the hammer at this sale; the preliminary bombshell which, to pursue Dibdin's metaphor, was the signal for a furious cannonade, consisted of the 'Biblia Sacra Græca,' printed by Aldus in 1518. This is the first complete edition of the Bible in Greek, and an important book on that account. It brought £4 15s., and any book-hunter might heartily pray for half a dozen copies now, on the same terms, for the present auction value runs to about six times as much. In fact, a sound copy sold only the other day for £27. So, too, Schoiffer's Latin Bible, printed at Mayence in 1472, folio, would be considered cheap now at £8 8s., assuming nothing was

A Comparison of Prices

wrong with it. In 1893 a copy in oak boards brought £20 exactly. On the other hand, Baskerville's Bible, Cambridge, 1763, was excessively dear at £10 15s., seeing that a very fair copy can be got at the present time for about £1 10s. Collectors of Bibles are responsible for much of the terrible confusion that takes place when we begin to draw comparisons in matters of filthy lucre. If a Bible come from a noted press, or is an original edition of its version, or very old indeed, then up goes the price, especially if it be printed in English. One would have thought that Baskerville being an Englishman, and a fine printer in his way, would have been good for much more than £1 10s. But no; he has not been dead long enough, for the collectors have made it a rule that no English Bible printed after 1717 is any good at all, and consequently that the 'Vinegar Bible' is the last book of the kind in point of date worth looking at, unless, indeed, exception be made in favour of one of the six large-paper copies of Bentham's Cambridge Bible of 1762, which are reported to have luckily escaped a conflagration. The late Mr. Dore, who was a strong man on the subject of old Bibles, says that a little research would reveal the existence of many more than the traditional half-dozen copies, so perhaps, after all, the conflagration is a myth. But if Baskerville's Bible brought what we should now consider to be an outrageous sum, what shall be said of 'The Holy Bible, illustrated with

Prints, published by T. Macklin, six volumes, folio, 1800,' which went for £43, incomplete though it was. Some £2 10s. for the whole seven volumes is not at all an uncommon auction price at the present day, and this amount and more would most certainly be swallowed up by the binding alone. What it comes to is that among all these books of theology, Biblical comment, criticism, polemics, sermons, and works of the Fathers, prices have fallen since 1812, except in those cases where collectors have stepped in to rescue old Bibles, works associated with some great religious revolution, or specimens of rare typography from the presses of old and noted printers.

For instance, there was here another Caxton called 'The Prouffytable boke for Mane's Soul,' folio, described as 'a beautiful copy,' which went for £140, and 'A Lytell Treatyse called Lucydarye,' 4to., Wynkyn de Worde, which brought £10. During the last dozen years the former book has appeared twice. At the Earl of Aylesford's sale in March, 1888, it brought (in company with 'The Tretyse of the Love of Jhesu Christ,' by Wynkyn de Worde, 1493) £305, and in July, 1889, an inferior copy, badly wormed, sold for £100.

These are the sort of books beloved by large public libraries, which are fast swallowing up the few that remain. From a pecuniary point of view it would perhaps pay some rich book-hunter of the Lenox type to buy up everything of the kind he could lay his hands on, though the worst of speculations such as these is that the interest on the money invested has a tendency to swell the principal, and so to add enormously to the original cost.

Among books that have gone down in price since the Duke of Roxburghe made his famed collection are those classical works of the ancients which were at that time all the rage. Virgil is no longer a name to conjure with, unless he happen to rank as a sound copy of the *editio princeps*. The first edition of Virgil was printed by Sweynheym and Pannartz at Rome, without date (1469?), and the Duke, notwithstanding the search of a lifetime, never came across a copy of that. Not more than seven copies can now be traced, and only two of these have come to the hammer for more than a hundred years. One, though imperfect, realized 4,101 francs at the La Vallière sale held at Paris in 1784, and the other £590 at the Hopetoun House sale at London in February, 1889. Then Homer is also a most desirable companion if he happen to have been printed at Florence, in two volumes, folio, 1488. About £100 is his price under those circumstances. Speaking generally, however, unless the printer comes to the rescue of a Greek or Latin classic, it may fairly be said to have fallen on an unappreciative generation. Scores upon scores of volumes, the very flowers of classic days, edited by Cunningham, Heyne, Porson, and other firstrate scholars of the last century, are to be met with in this bulky catalogue at sums varying from £2 to £3 each. In an old book of this class, a copy of Epictetus, edited by Heyne, and published at Dresden in 1756, was a slip of paper with a memorandum of the price at which it had been purchased in 1760. It was a bookseller's bill for £1 12s., made out to one 'Mr. Richard Cosgrove,' doubtless a good customer in his day. I have the book now, and it cost me fourpence, as much as it was worth. At the Duke of Roxburghe's sale a copy of this same edition brought £1 4s. This, no doubt, is rather an extreme case, but it will serve to illustrate the general principle sought to be enunciated, namely, that eighteenth-century classics are, for the most part, but wastepaper, for the simple reason that only a comparatively small number of people can read them. The learning of the schools may be deep and thorough—to assert the contrary would be to offend many excellent scholars of our own day; but it is nevertheless extremely probable, to say the least, that there are more books of the kind than there is any demand for, and so they litter the stalls, braving the wind and rain, till they are rescued by the merest chance and given house-room for a brief space.

In the opinion of many collectors the word 'poetry' only embraces English verse of a certain period, or written by certain people. The Duke's library was particularly rich in ancient English verse, lyric and dramatic, and some of the prices realized were very high. Webbe's 'A Discourse of English Poetrie,' 4to., 1586, brought £64, and 'The Paradyse of Daintie Devises,' 4to., 1580, £55. A curious collection of some thousands of ancient ballads, in three large folio volumes, sold for £477 15s. This collection, which was stated to be the finest in England, was originally formed for the celebrated library of the Earl of Oxford in the beginning of the eighteenth century, and was even then supposed to excel the Pepys collection at Cambridge. It came from the Harleian Library, and was purchased and afterwards largely added to by the Duke, who managed to secure a ballad printed by Leprevik at Edinburgh in 1570, a ballad quoted in 'Hamlet,' of which no other copy was known to exist, and many other extraordinary rarities. Dibdin was present when the 'poetry' was competed for, and bought several hundred pounds' worth of books, either on his own or somebody else's account, the whole of which he could easily have stowed away in his capacious pockets.

Naturally enough, the works of Shakespeare would first be turned to by anyone who held this catalogue in his hand for the first time. There are nearly three pages of closely printed entries referring to the great dramatist, and the only conclusion that can be arrived at is that in 1812 the early quartos must have been, if not exactly common, at any rate of no great rarity. It would be impossible to argue that Shakespeare was not then appreciated, for the contrary is well known to have been the fact. The late Mr. Halliwell-Phillipps in after-years talked of picking up early quartos for a few shillings each, and lamented that, for some mysterious reason which he found himself unable to explain, they had suddenly become scarce. Very likely he himself had excited a keen desire to possess them in the breasts of those who read his numerous books, or —publish it not in Gath !—the bulk of them may have fallen into unappreciative hands, and been used to light the fires withal.

However this may be, the early Shakespearian quartos, now of great price, were disposed of at the Roxburghe sale for only a little more, and occasionally for less, than the first editions of Marlowe, Massinger, and several other of the chief Elizabethan dramatists. A copy of the first folio sold, it is true, for £100, but the second only brought £15, the third £35, and the fourth £6 6s. This record, in the face of £84 for Boydell's edition in nine volumes, folio, 1802—a work which may now be expected to sell for £5 or £6, even with some of the illustrations after Smirke and others in proof state—is most extraordinary.

But let us get to the quartos and compare the prices of then and now. The first-named are those realized at the Roxburghe sale; those in brackets are modern, and authenticated with dates and items complete. There is more scope for reflection here, and a whole volume might be written on the mutability of fashion. 'Much a-doe about Nothing,' first edition, 4to., London, 1600, £2 17s. (the Gaisford sale, April 23, 1890, £130); 'A Midsommer Night's Dreame,' first edition, 4to., 1600, £3 3s. (*ibid.*, £116); 'The Merchant of Venice,' by Roberts, first edition, 4to., 1600, £2 14s. (the Cosens sale, November 11, 1890, £270); 'Pericles, Prince of Tyre,' 4to., 1619, 5s. (the Lakelands Library, March 12, 1891, £37); 'Pericles, Prince of Tyre,' 4to., 1635, 14s. (*ibid.*, £15); 'Romeo and Juliet,' second, or first complete edition, 4to., 1599, £12 12s. (the Perkins sale, July 10, 1889, £164); 'King Lear,' 4to., 1608, £6 12s. (the Brayton-Ives sale, New York, March 5, 1891, $425); 'Sir John Oldcastle,' first edition, 4to., 1600, 19s. (the Gaisford sale, April 23, 1890, £46).

These modern prices are small in comparison with what might have been, for none of the copies above mentioned were in the finest condition. If we want first-rate records we must go further back—to the Daniell sale, for instance, held in 1864, when thousands of pounds were paid as a matter of course for a selection of these little quarto volumes, which had successfully eluded the greasy fingers of generations of playgoers, the fires of disgusted Puritans, and the ignorance of our own people. Never shall we see nearly three thousand distinct lots of English poetry as previously defined disposed of at one single sale again, never again will prices rule so low. Many of these books are not to be met with at all in our generation, no matter what price may be offered for them, seeing that, as an old book-hunting friend used to say, they have become 'scandalously uniquitous.'

In addition to early English texts, the great Duke had amassed a splendid collection of romances of the Quixotic school, known in polite circles as the *Table Ronde*. He was not content, it seems, with the printed editions, but also collected many manuscripts on vellum, illustrated with beautiful illuminations. Among these curious manuscripts were several which had been used and translated by the celebrated Walter de Mapes for the entertainment of his Sovereign, Henry II. The printed books of this character, some of which occasionally, though very rarely, gladden the hearts of romantic bibliophiles, included the twenty-four small volumes recounting the exploits of Amadis of Gaul, published at Lyons and Paris in 1577, etc., and also several duplicates, £16 16s. A fairly good set, without the duplicates, brought £4 4s. in April, 1887—a dreadful drop, considering the demand there is for books of the kind. Still, this particular work has undoubtedly fallen, for another copy produced only £6 the June following. Nor, should I imagine, would 'L'Histoire du Noble Chavelier Berinus,' a quarto book printed at Paris, without date, sell for as much as £7 7s. at the present time, or 'Le Livre de Beufves de Hautonne,' folio, Paris, 1502, for £13 13s., or

A Comparison of Prices 27

'L'Histoire Merveilleuse du Grand Chan de Tartarie,' folio, 1524, for £22.

The twelve pages devoted to the enumeration of works of chivalry and romance glow with the martial achievements of Palmerin of England, Godeffroy de Boulion, Perceforest, Roy de la Grande Bretaigne, Perceval le Galloys, and scores of other champions who went about rescuing damsels in distress, sleeping in enchanted castles, and challenging the whole civilized race of men, one at a time, to mortal combat. Perceforest, by the way, in six folio volumes, Paris, 1528, went for £30, a fact worthy of note, inasmuch as another copy sold, a few months ago, for £10 10s. Of all the knights of ancient days, the regal Perceforest was the least worthy of credence, which is saying a great deal. His folios bristle with dragons, necromancers of the worst type, heroic rescues, combats with giants, devils, and all kinds of monsters who strove, and in vain, to destroy this past-master of Quixotic enterprise. That such books did at one time exercise considerable influence over adventurous spirits is undoubted. They were the only novels of the day, the only bit of light reading to be had in the interval between one tourney and another.

Passing by a large and almost complete collection of the separately published works of Robin Greene, that unfortunate who bought a groat's worth of wit with a million of repentance, we come to the Voyages and Travels, and note, as before, the differences in prices. Hakluyt's 'Collection of Voyages,' 2 vols., folio, 1589-99, brought £4 14s. 6d. (the Holding sale, January 17, 1895, £16; the Langham sale, June 19, 1894, £375, second edition, 3 vols., folio, which contained the map by Molyneux, of which only twelve copies are known. This copy belonged to the first issue, without the cartouche about Sir Francis Drake, which was subsequently added); 'Hakluytus Posthumus; or, Purchas his Pilgrimes,' 5 vols., folio, 1625-26, £42 (the Toovey sale, February 26, 1894, £51); 'Sir Francis Drake Revived,' 1652, and 'The World Encompassed by Sir Francis Drake,' 1652, the two pieces 7s. (the Hawley sale, July 2, 1894, £6 5s.); 'Cooke's Voyages,' 8 vols., 4to., 1773-84, with the large plates bound in two folio volumes, £63 (December 5, 1893, at Christie's, £3 12s., and on many other occasions for about the same amount); Eden's 'History of Travayle in the West and East Indies,' London, 1577, £6 10s. (the Thornhill sale, April 15, 1889, £10 5s.; the Wimpole Sale, June 29, 1888, £18 10s., original binding); Vancouver's 'Voyage of Discovery to the North Pacific Ocean,' 3 vols., 4to., and folio atlas of plates, 1798, £8 18s. (the Holding sale, January 17, 1895, £5 5s.). It would be more than tedious to pursue this comparative analysis further. Suffice it to say that as a rule the prices realized in 1812 for books of travel were greater than would be realized now under similar circumstances,

A Comparison of Prices 29

especially when the journeys undertaken were about the foot-worn Continent of Europe or in the various English counties. Pennant's 'Journey from Chester to London,' for example, is now a book of small account, yet the Duke of Roxburghe's copy sold for £7 15s.

Works relating to America are, curiously enough, almost absent from the Duke's catalogue, and it may fairly be taken for granted that at the beginning of the present century no one cared much about them. This will explain the extreme scarcity of many of these books now, for what people think lightly of they take no care to preserve. Hundreds and thousands of *Americana* must have been torn to fragments or otherwise destroyed in past days. Often of small size, they would escape the notice of lovers of folios, nor is their general appearance sufficiently imposing to appeal to those who value a book strictly in proportion to its external beauty. The Duke had only a few works of travel in any way relating to America, and as the list may be interesting, I have thought it best to transcribe it *verbatim et literatim*:

Schmidel 'Navigatio in Americam,' 4to., *Norib.*, 1599, £1 6s.

Las Casas's 'Discoveries, etc., of the Spaniards in America,' *Lond.*, 1699, 3s. 6d.

'History of the Bucaniers of America,' 4to., *Lond.*, 1684, £2 6s.

Hennepin's 'Discoveries in America,' 8vo., *Lond.*, 1698, 3s.

'Voyage dans l'Amerique,' par La Hontan, 2 vols., 8vo. *La Haye*, 1703, and 'Dialogues avec un Sauvage de l'Amerique,' par La Hontan, 8vo., *Amst.*, 1704, the two volumes 7s. 6d.
Hontan's 'Voyages to North America,' 2 vols., 8vo., *Lond.*, 1735, 6s. 6d.
Joutel's 'Voyage to the Missisippi,' 8vo., *Lond.*, 1714, 4s.
Jones' 'Present State of Virginia,' 8vo., *Lond.*, 1724, 2s.
Carver's 'Travels in N. America,' with plates, 8vo., *Lond.*, 1778, 10s.
Long's 'Voyages and Travels in N. America,' 4to., *Lond.*, 1791, 11s. 6d.
Mackenzie's 'Voyages in N. America,' 4to., *Lond.*, 1801, £1 6s.
Martyr's 'Historie of the West Indies,' 4to., *Lond.*, 1612, £3 7s.
'Histoire des Antilles,' par Père du Tertre, 3 vols., 4to., *Paris*, 1667, etc., £2 2s.
Blome's 'Description of Jamaica,' etc., 8vo., *Lond.*, 1678, 8s.
Gage's 'Travels in America and the W. Indies, 8vo., *Lond.*, 1699, 2s. 6d.
Wafer's 'Description of the Isthmus of America,' 8vo., *Lond.*, 1699, 9s.
'Collectio Peregrinationum in Indiam Orientalem et in Indiam Occidentalem, 19 partibus comprehensa, cum multis figuris Fratrum De Bry, 4 vols., folio, *Francof.*, 1519, £51 9s.

A Comparison of Prices

This 'Collectio Peregrinationum,' or Grands Voyages of Theodore de Bry, nearly always makes its appearance in the auction-room in sections. Nine of the parts, including the Additamentum, all first editions, with the plates and maps, sold on July 1, 1895, for £18 10s.

And now we must take a final leave of the Duke of Roxburghe and the collection which he got together during the course of a long life of painstaking and critical research. His catalogue is worth comparing with several important records of the present day, but to do this thoroughly would involve a tabulated analysis quite out of keeping with a work such as I am engaged upon. There is magic in comparisons, for they tell us what to avoid, and it may be that by their aid we could in a measure take fashion by the forelock and jump the years to come. Such a consummation is possible, but life is rounded too narrowly by the present, and therefore too short to make it worth anyone's while to endeavour to peep into futurity.

CHAPTER III.

SOME LUCKY FINDS.

THE book-hunter whose heart is in his quest never tires of tales of lucky discoveries, and of rare books bought for a song. This is natural enough, and, moreover, authentic details of some great find invariably stimulate his eagerness, and encourage him to persevere in the search for what he is repeatedly being told—as though he of all men did not know it already—is only to be met with casually, and by the merest of accidents. Now that all of us have settled among ourselves what books are rare, and desirable to possess on that account, as well as for many other reasons, everyone is, of course, naturally anxious to obtain the credit and still more the solid advantages of a startling discovery. It is each man for himself, and that perhaps is the reason why book-men of the old school invariably dressed in staid and sober black, like Sisters of Charity, to show the world at large that charity in matters that relate to their pursuit is dead. What man among the whole fraternity would give away his

Some Lucky Finds

suspicions that, in such and such a place, something may lie hidden? Rather would he make his way to the spot, in fear lest some other explorer might not, after all, have forestalled him, and during his journey there look to the right and the left of him, and get lost in crowds, as part of a deep design to shake off any other bookworm who, knowing his hunting instincts and great experience, might perchance be shadowing his footsteps. It has, indeed, been seriously questioned more than once by learned divines whether any collector, and more especially a collector of books, can by any possibility reach the kingdom of heaven, seeing that the inestimable gift of charity is by him regarded of such little account that he would do anything rather than practise it. It were best, however, to leave such polemical discussions to those who take an interest in them, and content ourselves with saying that the bookman's ways are necessarily tortuous, and his route through life circuitous.

It is next to impossible to open any book about books without meeting with instances of lucky finds, and the most curious part of the matter is that the stories are invariably more or less the same. Like the literary man's collection of stock phrases, which he uses with or without variation as occasion may require, and at judicious intervals, so these records of the chase strike us as being peculiarly liable to recur. From their opening sentences we know them—nay, the very mention

of a place or a name is often sufficient to make
an adept take up his parable and finish the narra-
tion. Let a man but whisper Hungerford Market,
and we know that he is going to tell us of the
fishmonger's shop where about half a century ago
'autograph signatures of Godolphin, Sunderland,
Ashley, Lauderdale, Ministers of James II.;
Accounts of the Exchequer Office, signed by
Henry VII. and Henry VIII.; Wardrobe Accounts
of Queen Anne; Secret Service Accounts, marked
with the "E. G." of Nell Gwynne; a treatise on
the Eucharist, in the boyish hand of Edward VI.;
and a disquisition on the Order of the Garter in
the scholarly writing of Elizabeth,' were rescued
from the eaters of fried plaice, and the tender
mercies of the barbaric tradesman who supplied
them. Mr. Rogers Rees, of 'Diversions of a
Bookworm' fame, got this story from somewhere,
though he perhaps would not know it now, for it
has been altered and added to in a score or more
of competing publications. Then there are stories
of Resbecque, who had a nose for a book second
to that of no hound for a fox, of Naudé, Colbert,
the great Pixérécourt, and many more. It would
be a shame to dish up these *plats* again, for
to make them palatable they would have to
be seasoned with imaginative details—an objectionable, not to say fraudulent, practice at its
best.

There is one story, however, which must be
raked up, and then decently buried again, for it is

Some Lucky Finds 35

to be hoped that we shall hear no more of it. It is perhaps not so well known as many of the rest, but in any case would not be mentioned here except as an almost unique illustration of the vicissitudes to which any book, however scarce and valuable it may be, is occasionally liable. It is, stripped of its glosses, to the following effect: When the library at Thorneck Hall was weeded of its superfluous books, the butler, who superintended the operation, came across a perfect copy of Dame Juliana Berners' 'Boke of St. Albans,' printed by an unknown typographer in 1486. One would have thought that the quaintness of the type, to say nothing of the extraordinary character of the coloured coats of arms and other illustrations, would at least have prompted inquiry; but no! it was thrown lightly aside, and in due course disposed of to a pedlar for ninepence. He in his turn sold it to a chemist at Gainsborough for four times the amount, and the chemist got £2 for his bargain from a bookseller, who, notwithstanding the fact that a very imperfect copy had been disposed of at the Duke of Roxburghe's sale many years before, positively sold it to another bookseller for £7. He, at any rate, was somewhat better informed, though not much, for once more the volume changed hands, this time to Sir Thomas Grenville, for £80. These transactions did not take place in the Middle Ages, but in the forties of the present century, and the wonder is that anyone with the slightest knowledge of books could have flown in the face of Dibdin's valuation of £420, which was at the time a matter of common knowledge. The butler may be honestly forgiven, and the pedlar commiserated with, the chemist even excused; but the two booksellers have no hope of redemption. The imperfect Roxburghe copy brought £147, and was resold at the White Knights sale for £84. In 1882 a perfect copy made its appearance at Christie's, and was knocked down for £630, being about a third less than the purchaser had made up his mind to pay for it had circumstances compelled. The life of a book is more often than not like the life of a horse. You use it, and little by little strip it of its value till it becomes a wreck and can be used no more. The 'Boke of St. Albans,' in company with many other treasured volumes, is not, however, for use, but a thing of sentiment, with a value that will probably continue to increase, till the leaves crumble before the touch of time.

Stories such as this are the book-man's tonic; they pick him up from the despondency into which he has fallen through lack of sustenance, and encourage him to believe that extreme scarcity is not always the reason of failure, but rather that all things come at last to him who can work and can wait, as indeed they do, for instances of good luck in the matter of discovering books, though perhaps not numerous when personal experience alone is considered, are

Some Lucky Finds 37

common enough in the aggregate. Here is a comparatively recent instance of good fortune:

In the summer of the year 1893 a London bookseller, who must be nameless, was offered a small library, then stored in a provincial town some thirty miles away. The owner copied the title-pages of a few of the books, and these were of such a character that the bookseller went over and eventually paid the price asked. What that amount was I am unable to state, but have good reason to suppose that it was less than £50. The majority of the volumes were, as is usually the case with old-fashioned and not particularly noticeable libraries, almost worthless. There were sermons preached in the long-ago to sleeping congregations, tracts and pamphlets on nothing in particular, an old and well-thumbed Prayer-Book or two of no importance, and the usual ponderous family Bible in tarnished gilt. On a casual survey, the whole of the books might have passed muster at a third-rate auction, and yet the bookseller was only too glad to see them safely housed in London. The reason was this: Among the refuse were *Americana*, some of extreme rarity, such as those who deal in such books are perpetually on the look-out for, and rarely find, even at their full value. As these books were publicly sold the following December, we are in a position to see what the bookseller got in return for his money, which, as I have said, was probably less than £50. The prices realized are given, so that there may be no mistake about the matter :

1. An Act for Exportation of Commodities, Incourage Manufactures, Trade, Plantations, four sheets, printed on one side only, in Black Letter, 1657, 8vo. £1 10s.
2. Hakluyt's Principal Navigations, Voyages, Traffiques, and Discoveries of the English Nation, 3 vols. in 2, Black Letter, 1599-1600, folio. £6 5s.
3. Josselyn's Account of Two Voyages to New England, 1674, 12mo. £6 15s.
4. Gabriel's Historical and Geographical Account of the Province and Country of Pennsilvania, and of New Jersey, 1698, 12mo. £31.
5. The Book of the General Lawes and Liberties concerning the Inhabitants of Massachusets, 1658. Printed according to the order of the Court, Cambridge (Mass.), 1660, small folio. £109.
6. Heath's A Journal of Travels from New Hampshire to Caratuck, on the Continent of North America, 1706, 4to. £5 15s.
7. Frampton's Joyfull Newes out of the Newfound Worlde, 1596, 4to. £4 15s.
8. Brereton's Briefe and True Relation of the Discoverie of the North Part of Virginia, 1602, 4to. £179. This copy had a few leaves mended.
9. Captain John Smith's Description of New England, 1613, 4to. £5.
10. Mourt's Relation or Journal of the Beginning

Some Lucky Finds 39

and Proceedings of the English Plantation Settled at Plimoth in New England, 1622, 4to. £40. Title and corner of the first leaf mended.
11. A Briefe Relation of the Discovery and Plantation of New England, 1622, 4to. £40.
12. Captain Thomas James's Strange and Dangerous Voyage in his intended Discovery of the North-West Passage, 1633, 4to. £17.
13. A Relation of Maryland, together with a Map of the Country. These Bookes are to be had at Master William Deasley, Esq., his house on the back side of Drury Lane, neere the Cockpit Playhouse; or, in his absense, at Master John Morgan's House in High Holborne, over against the Dolphin, London, Sept. 8, A.D. 1635. £76. This copy had the rare map.
14. Captain Luke Fox. North-West Fox, or Fox from the North-West Passage, 1635, 4to. £18.
15. Castell's A Short Discoverie of the Coast and Continent of America, 1644, 4to. £17.
16. Morton's New England's Memorial, printed at Cambridge (Mass.), 1669, 4to. £47.
17. Lederer's Discoveries in Three Several Marches from Virginia to the West of Carolina, 1672, 4to. £36.

And a few others, realizing a grand total of £658 odd for twenty-four works.

This remarkable collection of books of American interest is probably the most important that has

ever been met with in such a way. It may have
been formed a couple of centuries ago by someone
who took a burning interest in the 'New-found
Worlde,' as old Frampton calls America, and for
various reasons was unable to go there. Or it
may be that it was got together at a later date,
as the presence of Heath's 'Journal of Travels'
seems to suggest, by some bookish prophet, with
an eye to the main chance. If so, it is a pity that he
did not live long enough to reap the reward of his
foresight and energy, though, after all, even had
he done so, *cui bono*? Suppose he gave £5 for
the whole collection a hundred years ago—and
surely this is on the right side, for Hakluyt's
'Principal Navigations' would itself be worth as
much in those days—even then he would be woefully out of pocket for his pains, for his £5 would,
at compound interest, have increased to the best
part of £2,500. It is this little matter of interest
that upsets all calculations, and makes us all lying
prophets, so far as money is concerned.

Another extremely fortunate find was made, in
1896, in Hampshire. Can such things be? Can
any man be born to such a heritage of luck? It
seems that Mr. M. H. Foster, who recently bought
the Cams Hall estate in the county named, took
it into his head to explore the mansion, and in
doing so came across a number of old volumes
which had been abandoned by the late proprietor.
They lay, dusty and cobwebbed, in an old cup-
board, and instead of consisting of forgotten

Some Lucky Finds

ledgers and day-books, as would have been the case if any less fortunate gentleman had been concerned, proved to be of the greatest value. There was Caxton, writ large, among them—several Caxtons in fact, one being 'Justinian's Law,' such an exceedingly scarce book that a later edition once sold in London for £1,000—so at least it is said, though I have no record of the circumstance. At any rate, there is very little doubt that the volume in question would bring that amount or near it, and again let it be asked, Can any mortal living enjoy such favour from the gods? As in the case of the Thorneck Hall 'Boke of St. Albans,' so in that of the Cams Hall 'Justinian's Law'; how can such books be overlooked? Their very type betrays them sufficiently, one would think, to make it impossible for anyone, however careless, to pass them by.

Wholesale and very valuable discoveries like these are naturally of such infrequent occurrence that when one is made the news of it is disseminated far and wide, and commented upon in all the newspapers, which are nothing now if not literary, at least to some extent. Isolated finds, the picking up of some single object of interest or value, is the most the book-man reasonably hopes for in these days, and so long as he confines his desires within such narrow bounds it is hard indeed if he never reap an occasional success, such as that reported of a Melbourne gentleman, who only a few months ago picked out of a box labelled 'Fourpence each' a first edition of 'Sordello,' with an inscription in the handwriting of the author himself. Browning had written on the flyleaf, 'To my dear friend, R. H. Horne, from R. B.,' which, though certainly autographically less important than if he had signed his name in full, is yet a very pretty and cheap souvenir of an eminent poet. This R. H. Horne, who was himself a versifier, and once celebrated as the author of 'Orion,' emigrated to Australia in 1852, and became a Goldfields Commissioner at Ballarat. When he left there and came to England again, the book must have been left to the mercies of the Melbourne streets, in which presumably it existed till rescued from the low depth of misery which the miscellaneous box is supposed to imply.

Amongst a lot of old paper recently received at a mill in Andover, Connecticut, was a Bible which some Goth had sold by weight. In it was an inscription, 'This Bible was used in the pulpit by Rev. Stephen West, pastor in Stockbridge, Mass., from 1759 to 1818.' This book was perhaps not so important from a worldly point of view as 'The Art of Cookery made Plain and Easy; By a Lady,' which the late Mr. Sala rescued from oblivion in the Lambeth Marshes, as will shortly be related; but the Rev. Stephen West was a very noted personage in his day, and there are hundreds of people, more particularly in America, who would be very glad to possess a memorial of him. He was the author of the well-known 'Essay on Moral Agency,' 1794, the 'Sketches of the Life of the Rev. S. Hopkins,' 1805, and other books which in their day enjoyed a very extensive circulation.

Mr. Sala's discovery of Mrs. Glasse's cookery-book was due to his habit of prowling round the old bookstalls of the Metropolis, particularly those which line the narrow streets of Lambeth Marshes and the New Cut. On a Sunday morning these places are like a fair, and, literally, scores of peripatetic booksellers, who for the most part follow another occupation the remaining days of the week, take their stand with barrows piled high with lore. The mob pull the volumes about, and haggle over the prices, so that the stock displayed is not, on the whole, in the best possible condition. Still, sometimes you do meet with a well-preserved rarity, as Mr. Sala did when he purchased 'The Art of Cookery made Plain and Easy,' 1747, thin folio, for six humble pennies. He had the book bound by a first-rate craftsman, and when it came at last to the inevitable hammer some two or three years ago, it sold for £10, and was reasonably worth considerably more. Only five or six copies of this edition are known to be in existence, but of the second edition, which also appeared in 1747, only one copy is known, according to the Rev. Richard Hooper, whose unique specimen contains an inscription worth reproducing. It runs as follows :

' Steal not this Book my honest Frend for Fear the Galowss should be your hend and when you Die the Lord will say and wares that Book you stole away.'

Cooks are proverbially greasy people, and a book passing through their hands is apt to return like 'Tom and Jerry' from those of a prize-fighter or sporting publican. Still, 201 persons subscribed to the first edition of Mrs. Glasse, and 282 to the second, and some were neither cooks nor publicans, but members of the aristocracy, who might be expected to treat their books with some show of respect. But perhaps they expressly bought them for the use of their cooks, and handed them over to the kitchen authorities, in which case their rarity is accounted for. All old cookery-books, and not merely Mrs. Glasse's famous work, are rare, because they are books of practical utility meant to be consulted in a republic of pots and pans, and grease and litter; but Mrs. Glasse's guide is more desirable than most other English books of the kind, because there is a sentiment hanging around it like a halo, by reason of words which are *not* to be found therein, 'First catch your hare.'

For my part, whenever I see a cookery-book flaunting it on a street barrow, I rescue it at once, for I have a belief, rightly or wrongly, that some of these days there will be a very great demand for old works of the kind. There is a present disposition to return to ancestral dishes, which

Some Lucky Finds   45

means the resuscitation of 'The Skilful Cook,' 'The Good Housewife's Jewel,' 'The Queen's Closet Opened,' 'The Ladies' Practice,' and many other volumes where the necessary recipes are to be found. For some time past, indeed, recipe-books of all kinds have practically disappeared from the stalls where once they were so numerous. 'They're miking a lot of 'em hup at the West Hend,' said a stall proprietor, jerking his thumb in the direction of Belgravia, from which it must be understood, not that any manufactory of forgeries is as yet established there, but merely that the upper ten think a great deal of old recipe-books, and are buying them up for their cooks to practise with.

It is sadly to be feared that the paper-mills grind many good books exceeding small at times. This is to be conjectured by reason of the fact that every now and then a consignment is stopped and rescued just as it is about to be transformed into pulp. What happens once, is, we may be sure, repeated at intervals, though direct evidence may be wanting to convict the paper-maker. Evidence of this character is, however, occasionally forthcoming, as, for example, in the case of the sixth volume of Dr. Vallancey's 'Collectanea de Rebus Hibernicis,' which was published in two divisions in 1804. The previous five volumes are comparatively common, but both parts of volume six are very scarce, nearly all the copies having been accidentally sold for waste-paper, and treated as such. Charles Dickens's 'Village Coquettes' and also Swinburne's 'A Song of Italy' were once much rarer books than they are now, and commanded a great deal more money in the market. Neither book sold well when published, and a very considerable 'remainder' was stacked in quires in the publishers' cellars. One day these Augean stables were cleaned out, and the 'Village Coquettes' and 'A Song of Italy' were saved from the mill by the merest of accidents, with the result that the former book went down fifty per cent. in the market, and the latter to next to nothing. These finds were noised abroad, with the result that they were robbed of most of their importance. Imagine, if we can, a great discovery of a hundred copies of Shakespeare's first folio. And imagine also a journal of credit getting hold of the news and noising it abroad, as it would do when it had satisfied itself that there was at least a substratum of truth in the story. The result we know. Half the value of the find would vanish away on the instant, and rightly so, too, as a strict moralist would doubtless insist.

Sometimes, though not often, some of the literary auctioneers will make a mistake, and in the most unaccountable manner include a rarity in a 'parcel' of rubbish. A good copy of the first edition of Cocker's 'Decimal Arithmetic,' 1685, was picked up in this way a short time ago, though not in London, and at Leeds a

Some Lucky Finds 47

dealer bought an original and very interesting letter in Shelley's autograph, which had somehow or other slipped among a number of schoolbooks of trifling value. It is the easiest thing in the world to make a mistake where books are concerned, more particularly when they consist of pamphlets and other works which lie in a small compass. Folios can take care of themselves, but a man needs to have a first-rate all-round knowledge who would essay to catalogue a good old-fashioned miscellaneous library.

In France, sale-catalogues are prepared by experts, who are called in to assist the auctioneers; in London the auctioneers keep their own cataloguers, and in the country towns they seek the assistance of booksellers, or do the work themselves. If a sale is advertised to be held at a house where furniture is the chief attraction, the presence of a comparatively small number of books acts like a magnet, and people are attracted from far and near in the hope that something good will fall to their share. Sometimes they are rewarded, more frequently not; for what everybody is looking for is almost sure to be detected by several, if it exist at all, and then, of course, the price is run up. Still, occasionally, a whole roomful of experts will miss a bargain which stares them in the face. Unaccountable as it may seem, I myself once bought for £1 a first-rate copy of Alken's 'National Sports of Great Britain,' 1821, a scarce folio book full of coloured plates. It was wedged in among a quantity of furniture, and had escaped observation, although there were several booksellers in the room.

The highest form of genius to be met with in book-men is, however, the capacity possessed by a very few of them to detect the author of an anonymous book by reference to the style in which it is written. If we happened to meet with 'Swellfoot the Tyrant' for a trifling sum, and passed it by, we should deserve our fate, for the authorship is so generally and widely known that there is no excuse for any book-man who is unacquainted with the facts surrounding it. But were we to discover another poem by Shelley, which no one had ever heard of before, and also be able to prove conclusively that he must, *ex necessitate*, have been the author of it, that indeed would be a triumph of skill. Some few books have been rescued in this way, 'Alaric at Rome,' for instance, which was discovered and assigned to Matthew Arnold simply and solely by reference to the style. 'Alaric at Rome' made a sensation when the authorship came to be known, and book-hunters were searching high and low, and giving commissions in hot haste. A few copies were unearthed in this way; but the number was xceedingly small, not more than two or three, I believe, and the pamphlet, for it is nothing more, is at this moment an object of deep interest to the few, who are in reality very many, when we come

Some Lucky Finds 49

to reflect that none but perhaps half a dozen can ever hope to possess it.

When we get into bookland, more particularly into that secluded corner of it where specialists assemble to compare notes and exhibit their treasures, confusion springs up on the instant. The specialist cannot always know his business thoroughly. If you mention a particular book which comes within his purview, he will probably tell you how many copies of it are known to exist, and where they are, how many of the total number are cropped, and to what extent, and whether the titles have been 'washed' or otherwise renovated. He knows accurately the original cost in money of each, and how much each would be likely to sell for in case it were brought to the hammer. All this is, of course, good and solid information, but it is too microscopically minute and exact to interest anyone outside a very small circle. To most of us these details are unimportant, and yet every lucky find must pass some specialist, who assigns to it its proper position in point of excellence, and makes it keep its place. For this reason I have been charged with the offence of speaking about him as though he were a common bookworm, ready to feed on anything that came in his way, which is, of course, flat treason, not by any means to be silently borne by the élite.

CHAPTER IV.

THE FORGOTTEN LORE SOCIETY.

COMMON-SENSE tells us that 'finds,' as they are popularly called, must necessarily be made by the purest of accidents. Valuables of any kind, though frequently lost or mislaid, seldom remain unappropriated for long, and to search for them with intent is to be too late in such a large preponderance of cases that it is not worth while to go to the trouble of doing so. A 'find,' as I take the word to mean in a popular sense, is the discovery of something of special interest or value, followed by its acquisition at a price which is, at market rates, very much less than it is worth. The price paid is the gist of the find in the popular eye, though there is no denying that, in the case of genuine literature, this is about the most unsatisfactory view that can be taken of the matter.

If an extremely scarce or interesting book, for which one has, perhaps, been searching for years, is at last acquired at any price whatever, the 'find' is none the less real, merely because the

The Forgotten Lore Society

cost is great, though we should have hard work to convince the ordinary book-buyer that this is so. He is of opinion that money can buy anything, books not excepted, and in that he is assuredly wrong, for there are many books which are not to be procured at any price, simply because they have disappeared as though they had never been. We know they once lived, because they are referred to by name in contemporary reviews, or have perhaps been reprinted; but now they are as dead as the 'Original Poetry' of Victor and Cazire, which can be traced to the pages of the *Morning Chronicle* of September 18, 1810, and to a couple of reviews of the day, but of which no copy is now known.

It was this 'Original Poetry' that first suggested the idea of a society to promote the systematic search for 'rare and curious volumes of forgotten lore,' as Edgar Poe felicitously has it. These poems were the production of Shelley and a friend —probably his cousin, Harriet Grove—but had hardly been published a week when Stockdale, the publisher, inspecting the book with more attention than he previously had leisure to bestow, recognised one of the pieces as having been taken bodily from 'The Monk.' Shelley then suppressed the entire edition in disgust, but not before nearly a hundred copies had been put into circulation. The question is, Where are these derelicts now? It is incomprehensible that all can have been consigned to the flames or torn to pulp.

Most probably one at least has survived the wrack of time and neglect, and may be lying perdu in the garret or rubbish-heap of some old farmhouse, in which Shelley is but little known, and 'Victor' and 'Cazire' absolute strangers both. And if this particular book, why not many others, which, though not absolutely lost, are yet so very rarely met with that it is the ambition of every book-hunter, great or small, to track them down?

As the world is not inhabited entirely by specialists, the inference is that books of all kinds, good as well as indifferent, lie hidden away in obscure places, waiting the coming of some appreciative explorer who will rescue them from the neglect of many years, and restore them to the world from whence they came. It is no use advertising in these cases. Every week, year in and year out, stereotyped advertisements appear in all sorts of likely and unlikely journals, and nothing ever seems to come of them. They are read, doubtless, by the very people whose goods and chattels stand in need of a thorough overhauling; but they do not know the real extent of their possessions, and usually have a fine contempt for articles of small bulk—a by no means unusual circumstance, be it said, even in educated circles, for it is on record that, when Sion College was burned down, many priceless volumes in the library were destroyed simply because the attendants, at the risk of their lives, devoted all the time available to the rescue of folios.

The Forgotten Lore Society 53

Thus it came to pass that Prynne's miscellaneous writings were for the most part saved, while other treatises, of far more importance, but smaller in size, were licked up by the flames, and so perished. The natural instinct of human beings is to place confidence in weight, and to ascribe wisdom to bulk. For centuries this idea prevailed throughout Europe, and doubtless prompted Nicolai de Lyra to write those hundreds of folios of commentary on the New Testament which at one time were the mournful heritage of thousands. So also the great Baxter reaped much renown by reason of his seventy folios or quartos, causing Bayle to remark, 'Perhaps no copying clerk who ever lived to grow old amidst the dust of an office ever transcribed so much as this author has written.'

The real book-hunter of to-day is, however, fortunately free of the ancient superstition, and knows very well that as a general rule the scarcest printed books are those which are small in size. To the people at large this is not so, and thus it is that pamphlets of extreme rarity, small volumes which you can hold in your hand with ease, or carry in an inner pocket with comfort, are neglected and eventually forgotten, and doubtless destroyed in sheer ignorance, more often than we care to think of. It was with the object of rescuing some of these that the Forgotten Lore Society first saw the light seven years ago. This, indeed, was not its real name, but the title is a good one, and as descriptive of the objects sought to be attained as any other that could be invented. The idea was to search the country for neglected books in the hope that something at least might be discovered among the heaps of ancestral rubbish that time and the elements are fast bringing to decay.

Now, I venture to state that the more anyone of impartial judgment considers facts and probabilities, the more he must be satisfied that this was no Quixotic scheme. In some instances it is plain that even the most protracted and thorough search would be mere waste of time, as, for instance, in the case of Byron's 'Fugitive Pieces,' 1806, which is known to have been entirely destroyed, with the exception of three copies, all of which can be accounted for. But, then, the operations of the society were not confined to odd volumes, but to rarities of any kind and in any number that Providence might see fit to throw in its way. If not Byron, then Shelley, or Burns, or those older authors whose very names are synonyms for extreme scarcity, such, for example, as Brereton, Whitbourne, W. Hamond, Bullinger, and the scores who have written seventeenth-century poems and composed old music to sing them to. Have all practically vanished, or are they merely under the lock of a combination of indifference and ignorance for a time ? That was the question.

With this society I was connected as an

The Forgotten Lore Society   55

ordinary member, and allotted a certain acreage over which to roam, on the distinct understanding that any advantage was to accrue to the benefit of the members as a whole. Elaborate rules were drawn up, and every imaginable contingency fully provided for. There was no lack of money, and no want of enterprise or enthusiasm; yet the project failed for the simplest of all reasons — but one which had apparently never entered into the calculations of the promoters. Spread over England, and some parts of Scotland and Ireland, were over a hundred book-men, all of them thoroughly well versed in literature of a certain kind, but, with few exceptions, rigorous specialists, who affected particular authors or subjects, and knew little outside the restricted circle they had made their own. Let any one of these be drawn within the vortex of his favourite branch of study, and I am sure that he would have acquitted himself admirably; but what was wanted in a matter of this kind was a general and extensive acquaintance with the market, and not a knowledge, however deep or profound, of the lives of authors long since dead, and of what they wrote, and the circumstances that attended the publication of their works. This, unfortunately, was the information with which most of the members set out to search the countryside, and the mistakes they made would be sufficient to excite the laughter of even the tyro were they but published. A perfect Iliad of woes tracked the footsteps of each member of this society wherever he went, and it is not at all surprising that it eventually languished and was finally dissolved. A few of these mistakes may, however, be set down with the object of showing how easy it is to tumble into error, and at the same time to be perfectly satisfied that the mistake, if any, is on the wrong shoulders.

Every collector of Mr. Ruskin's works knows that on December 14, 1864, he delivered a lecture at the Town Hall, Manchester, and that this lecture was printed and published in that city, in pamphlet form, under the title of 'The Queens' Gardens.' He is also aware that only three copies of the pamphlet are known to exist, and if he is very well informed indeed he will know who has them, and where they got them from, and at what price. A portion of this information was in the possession of a member at Bath, who, as he said, had accidentally discovered a copy of the 'book' in a parcel of odds and ends that was to be sold by auction the following day. In his letter he requested a reply by telegram first thing in the morning saying to what price he was to go, as he had reason to believe that other persons beside himself were aware of the circumstance. There was no time for explanations, so the wire was sent, though the word 'book' came with a very suspicious ring. It was as well perhaps that the limit was intentionally put low, or there is no telling to what absurd price the parcel of miscellanea might not have been forced by his eager-

The Forgotten Lore Society 57

ness. As it was, it was bought for £2 10s., or about six or seven times as much as it was worth, for 'The Queens' Gardens' was not the coveted pamphlet at all, but the book known as 'Sesame and Lilies' (and not even the first edition of that), published by Smith, Elder and Co. in 1865, which contains the reprints of the two lectures (1) 'Of Kings' Treasuries,' (2) 'Of Queens' Gardens.' It was evident that this sort of thing had only to become general and the society would be ruined, for all payments came from the common fund. When the error was pointed out, the member cavilled and argued, but could not be convinced. He was certain that he had bought the true and original 'Queens' Gardens,' and darkly hinted at secession.

On another occasion a member bought 'Friendship's Offering,' for 1840, merely because it contains 'The Scythian Guest.' He, too, could not be persuaded that the error was his rather than that of the bookseller who sold it him. Times without number one edition was mistaken for another; over and over again were imperfect or tattered volumes bought at prices that would have been impossible but for the London treasury of this secret society. 'No good comes,' says old John Hill Burton, 'no good comes of gentlemen buying and selling'—a dictum which was manifestly applicable here. Had the confident purchaser of 'Queens' Gardens' been confronted with Nichols's 'Herald and Genealogist,' he would have been in his element, for he was an adept in the lore of armorials and pedigrees, and had a fine collection of volumes of that kind. Outside these subjects he knew but little, which for all practical purposes is infinitely worse than knowing nothing at all.

Another grievous error resulted in the purchase of Shakespeare's ' Venus and Adonis,' 'The Rape of Lucrece,' ' The Passionate Pilgrim,' and ' Sonnets to Sundry Notes of Musick,' at a good round sum. The pieces were bound up together in dilapidated calf, and as each had a separate pagination there may have been just a shadow of excuse for the payment of £2, which was the price demanded. But this book was merely Lintott's first collected edition, a work which might have been manufactured expressly for the behoof of innocent purchasers, so antiquated and primitive does it look. Had it been Cote's collected edition of 1640, instead of Lintott's comparatively worthless, and certainly very careless, production, which he took good care not to date, all would have been well; but this was never at any time likely to be the case, for the price was dead against a supposition of the kind. Price is, indeed, often a most valuable guide to the real worth of a book; though this is not always the case, as the following anecdote of a circumstance that happened to myself abundantly proves. I took the greatest pains to trace every step in the history I am about to unfold, and know that the details are true.

The Forgotten Lore Society 59

It is the custom of many booksellers to send out their catalogues in alphabetical order, and had only my name been Abbot, or even Abrahams, this account of an accident which can hardly fade from my memory would probably have never been written. The Forgotten Lore Society would have reaped most of the benefit certainly, but, on the other hand, I should have been rich in the consciousness of having obtained for a mere trifle one of the finest known copies of an extremely rare piece, and one of the few of any quality that have ever come into the market at any price.

The society had not been in working order a month, when one of those extraordinary strokes of luck which often fall to the share of the gambler at the commencement of his career, and as certainly desert him at the end of it, happened to me. It was brought late one evening by a bookseller's catalogue which I, being much occupied at the time, threw aside till a more convenient season. They say that strange psychological influences often work out the destiny of men, although they know it not, and some such influence must have been haunting me then, for contrary to all custom, and notwithstanding the fact that to catch the last post was a matter of imperative necessity, I found that the catalogue had an altogether exceptional if not unique attraction. Do what I might, I could not forget its existence, nor could I make satisfactory progress with the work which had, whether I liked it or not, to be finished and out of the house half an hour before midnight at the latest. So the catalogue was opened, curiously enough, at a place at which there was no reason it should open, for after a while I lost it and had some difficulty in finding it again. It had opened, however, at page 8, and the first entry that caught my eye was this, word for word exactly:

114. Hornem (Horace) The Waltz: an Apostrophic Hymn. By Horace Hornem, Esq.: 4to., 1813, unbound. 3s. 6d.

Now, there are, of course, two early editions of 'The Waltz,' one the quarto above-named, and the other an octavo published in 1821, and it was quite likely, and indeed more than probable, that the bookseller, with his mind's eye fixed on the excessively scarce issue of 1813, might have unconsciously written it down instead of the comparatively common octavo. Another hypothesis suggested itself, namely, that the entry was designed to bring customers to his place of business, and that 'The Waltz' of 1813 had no existence there in fact. Such devices for making trade are not unknown, and this might very well be one of them. Nevertheless, I determined to test the matter, and though the laugh is greatly to my discomfort even at this distance of time, I do not mind admitting that I was, metaphorically speaking, glued to the doorstep long before the shop opened in the morning. To sit there in

The Forgotten Lore Society 61

reality I could not for shame, so I walked about Oxford Street within bowshot, ready to besiege the door in case any other snapper-up of unconsidered trifles should show an anxiety to forestall his brethren of the chase. Even when the shop opened, I did not walk in immediately, nor when there did I brutally ask point-blank for the coveted treasure. An uneasy conscience pointed out that, if there were anything in the matter, too great an anxiety might give rise to suspicion, and 'The Waltz' would in that case be difficult to find. I bought another book, which I did not want, and not till then suggested number 114.

'Gone,' said the clerk, looking at his copy of the catalogue.

'Gone?' said I.

'Yes,' he replied, ' sold yesterday.'

I thought at the time that a trace of a smile played about the corners of his mouth as he said this, and I should not wonder if that were so, for the bookseller afterwards told me that his place had been besieged for many days by hungry bookworms, who had sauntered in one after the other in the most careless manner imaginable, and asked for this very 'Waltz.' 'They positively danced on the pavement,' he said, 'when they found it had gone,' and with this small joke he was fain to mollify himself, for it was the literal truth that in an evil moment he had sold a pearl of great price for the beggarly sum of 3s. 6d. He did not know to whom; he had never seen the man before, and 'in all probability,' he added with a sigh, 'I shall never see him again.'

The subsequent history of one of the finest, if not the finest, copies of Byron's quarto 'Waltz' in existence is as follows: The original purchaser sold it to a dabbler in books for 10s., and he in his turn disposed of it for £4 to a man who, though not a bookseller, occasionally acted as such, and was thoroughly conversant with every move of the market. He had no difficulty in selling it by telegram, and the price paid—£60—was not, under the circumstances, in the least too high, for the copy was as fresh and clean as when it left the publishing offices of Sherwood, Neely, and Jones more than eighty years ago, and had not been tampered with in any way.

The suggestion that the price demanded for a book is often a test of its real worth is both proved and avoided by this story. As I did not, as it happened, secure the 'Waltz,' I feel sorry for the bookseller, and would point out to him that it is impossible for anyone, bookseller or not, to be acquainted with every volume and pamphlet that has ever been published. He made a mistake of such grave consequences to himself that he is not at all likely to make another of the same kind. His sin merely consisted in either not knowing who 'Horace Hornem, Esq.,' really was, or more probably in momentarily and yet irrevocably confusing that pseudonym with some other which he may have had in his mind at the time. This is a

The Forgotten Lore Society 63

very common source of error, and very probably accounts for the incident. On the other hand, the action of the intermediate holder in selling the book for £4 is inexplicable and inexcusable. Had he said 10s. 6d., and thus made 6d. on the transaction, he would have had the excuse of absolute ignorance in his favour, but £4 is such a curious and yet significant amount that there can be no question that he at any rate knew sufficiently well what he was about to make the absence of proper inquiry on his part a positive crime. Any such value as £4 placed on a pamphlet of twenty-seven pages is in itself such an indication of value that no anxious would-be purchaser of any scarce and yet insignificant-looking book dare offer anything like the amount for it. He must either pay the full price or near it, which is more honest, as well as more satisfactory in the long-run, or swallow his principles and tender next to nothing with a nonchalant air.

Personally I feel sorry that the Forgotten Lore Society had such a small measure of success, for it deserved well. The management was too vicarious for the times, and, moreover, its object was not the buying and selling of books, which one man, if he have sufficient capital, can do as well as twenty. To rescue mean-looking but valuable literature from almost certain destruction was its one and only study, and the realization of its dreams was only accomplished very partially, because, as I have hinted, the members of the association were specialists moving in narrow grooves. The few successes that can be placed to its credit would, however, have been its curse had it dealt hardly and uncharitably with the ignorant people who on more than one occasion parted with small fortunes (to them) for the price of a day's subsistence. To buy a perfectly clean copy of Thackeray's 'Second Funeral of Napoleon' for 2s. was a work of art, for the old woman who sold it, in order to buy tea, as it subsequently transpired, wanted more, and yet was so thoroughly saturated with suspicion that she would probably have refused to sell at any price had more been offered. The book was acquired for that sum, as I have said, after much discussion and with many misgivings, at least on one side; but when bought, the circumstances altered, and she found herself possessed of more money than she had had the control of at one time in her life before, for it is, I think, to the credit of the Forgotten Lore Society that it voluntarily paid into the Post-Office Savings Bank a sum of £10 to the order of the seller a few days after the transaction was carried through. Such finds as these were, however, few and far between. In nearly every case such books as the ignorant are possessed of are very inferior, and, what is perhaps not surprising, assessed by their owners at ridiculous prices.

It was part of the business of the society to advertise for books in country journals, and to

The Forgotten Lore Society 65

while away a few moments I give the gist or the actual text of some of the replies received. One correspondent wrote to say that he hadn't got no books, but would sell us a fox-terrier pup, if that would do instead, and then he proceeded to enumerate at great length what he called its 'pints,' concluding with the remark that he had sent it off that very evening by passenger train. It turned up, sure enough, in the morning, sorrowful of countenance, a snarling, disreputable cur, which we were only too glad to feed and return to its home without delay.

This was an instance, fortunately very rare, of the wilful substitution of one article for another of a totally different kind; but nearly every letter we took the trouble to answer proved to be misleading in one way or another, and not a few contained a series of palpable untruths. There would be no advantage in reproducing many of these epistles, and, moreover, the circumstances surrounding them are not of sufficient interest to warrant more than a passing notice. Suffice it to say that they were mere vendors' glosses, not to be taken *au sérieux*. The number of books with 'magnificent plates' or in 'splendid condition' that turned out on inspection to be the tramps and tatterdemalions of bookish society was very surprising. Some few, however, were very curious, and others so quaint in diction that I have no hesitation in copying them either wholly or in part. Here is one:

'Deer Sur i begs to state as ou i ave sume bukes their is Boosey anecdoates of fishin for wich five bob and a lang his hanglin skeches hopen to hoffers stackhouse new history of the Holy Bibel to pouns an a lot moar to order deer Sur if you be willin and i wil sen to luke at for 2£ on the nale your respectabul ——.'

A 'bob,' I may explain for the benefit of my American readers, is the slang equivalent of a shilling, or twenty-four cents.

The following reply, full of facetiousness and loaded with cunning, came from a village near Kirkby Stephen, in Westmoreland:

'SIR

'Seeing your advt in the *Gazete* I hasten to copie out the titles of some books which have been in my family for I dont know how long. A Bookseller come up from Lancaster last Toosday and wanted to have them sore but as I could see he wanted to cheat me I thought it better tell him so in plain English which is the way of yours truly who is a wrestling man and champion chucker out of these parts round about. Am open to good offer for the lot but will sell any at following and no discount. Ellicot Lectures on J. Christ, 10s. Durny Histoir de Romans, vol. 4, 6s. Stock Exchange year Book for 1884, 7s; Ante Baccus, a choise volume bound in calf, 17s. 6d. Scrope Days and Nights of Fishing 1843, 12s. The Female Parson 4s, and plenty

The Forgotten Lore Society

more too numerous till I see what you are made of. Please write at once if you want any.

'Yours truly ——.'

The upshot of this was that we said we should like to see Scrope and the 'Female Parson,' but our bellicose correspondent refused to part with either till he got the money, for he did not, he said, intend to trouble himself about useless references. So the money was sent, and in due course the books arrived, carriage not paid. The 'Female Parson,' which we had never heard of before, proved to be worthless, but Scrope's 'Salmon Fishing' was really a beautiful copy of the first edition in the original cloth, and this it was that had doubtless tempted the Lancaster bookseller.

Then there was a lady in Somersetshire who kept up a correspondence for over a month. She had a splendid copy, so she said, of Sturm's 'Reflections,' which she was ready to sell for 15s. In vain was she informed that the book was not of a kind to interest us; she knew better, and persistently lowered the price, 1s. at a bid, till her letters had in sheer desperation to be put in the waste-paper basket. We found ladies, as a rule, distressing correspondents, who flatly refused to be put off with a courteous negative. With them it was simply a question of price, and had we been persuaded by their blandishments, we should soon have had a cellar full of sermons, Gospel

Magazines, and all the rubbish that Time refuses to annihilate and men to buy.

One of the most extraordinary letters we ever received came from a clergyman in the Midlands, whose disgust for Pierce Egan and his school was so great that he had determined to sacrifice 'Tom and Jerry' for 20s.:

'DEAR SIR,

'I much regret troubling you with a book which has, to me, been a source of grievous disappointment, and positive danger to my children. How anyone could have written such a wicked history of debauchery and human extravagance is indeed surprising, and I have thought many a time of consigning it to the flames, so that in a measure it might follow its disreputable author. I allude to "Life in London; or the Day and Night Scenes of Jerry Hawthorn, Esq., and his Elegant Friend, Corinthian Tom, accompanied by Bob Logic, the Oxonian, in their Rambles and Sprees through the Metropolis," by Pierce Egan. This work has, I regret to say, been in my family for very many years—more than I care to count—and I would willingly part with it, although there is nothing I dislike so much as severing old associations, however much to my distaste they may be. If you like, I will dispose of the book for £1, which perhaps, from a marketable point of view, it may be worth.

'I am, dear sir,
  'Yours very truly ——.'

The Forgotten Lore Society 69

There is, of course, no denying that the morality of Jerry Hawthorn, Esq., and his elegant friend would have to be searched for in case its existence were seriously disputed; but it seems passing strange that so small a sum as 20s. should be able to smooth away all remembrance of the orgies of Drury Lane and the crapulence of its dirty gin vaults, cider cellars and night-houses, which had so mortally offended the worthy clergyman.

He was indeed quite right in removing the book from the reach of his children; but what about our morality, and that of the person to whom, for anything he knew to the contrary, we might sell Pierce Egan's free and easy romance? The book came, and proved, as was half suspected, to be Hotten's reprint of 1869, with which lovers of this class of literature will have nothing whatever to do.

Such are a few of the experiences of the Forgotten Lore Society in its efforts to rescue good but unfortunate books from the apathy of neglect. The object was a good one, though the reward was practically nil. Let us reflect for a moment that even the few books of antiquity which have come down to make us richer are for the most part imperfect, and we shall see the necessity of taking extreme care of the important ones that are written now, and of doing everything in our power to prevent their destruction at the hands of unappreciative owners.

The mere fact of printed books being published

in large quantities to the edition does not seem to affect the question of their existence in the long-run. All alike, good, bad, and indifferent, will go down the long road in time, and our descendants, more or less remote, will only hear of them in a casual and traditional way. Tacitus was one of the most popular Roman authors of his time, and yet he only lives to us in fragments, notwithstanding the fact that thousands upon thousands of copies of his 'History' were disseminated throughout the empire. Every public library in Rome was compelled to have at least one copy, and no fewer than ten transcriptions were made every year at the charge of the State. Plutarch wrote fourteen biographies that are missing now, and of 251 books quoted by him more than eighty are absolutely unknown. The Emperor Claudius wrote a 'History of the Etruscans,' which from the very nature of the case must have had a wide circulation; Julius Cæsar, a slashing criticism of Cato's life and acts; Lucullus, a history of the Marsi. All these have vanished. Of the forty plays of Aristophanes but eleven remain. Menander is unknown except by name, and Æschylus is in rags. Porphyry's diatribe against the Christians, the most important book of its kind that any Christian could have at his command, has vanished, and in all likelihood will never be restored.

Nor need we go to ancient Greece or Rome for such instances. Several poems by Shelley have completely disappeared already, and some

The Forgotten Lore Society 71

of Byron's have been, more than once, at their last gasp. Old English ballads and songs have been 'lost' by hundreds at a time, and nearly all the records dealing with the private life of Oliver Cromwell are missing. The story of Carlyle's 'Squire Papers' is a characteristic one, and distinctly to the point. While that author was laboriously collating the scraps of evidence relative to the great Protector that had survived the honest but mistaken zeal of triumphing Royalists, he received a letter from an unknown correspondent, who stated that he possessed a mass of Parliamentary documents, among them the diary of an ancestor, one Samuel Squire, a subaltern in the 'Stilton Troop' of Ironsides. The letter was accompanied by extracts from this diary and other papers, and went on to say that the writer, who had been brought up to regard Cromwell in the very worst possible light, and his own ancestor with shame as the aider and abettor of an atrocious crime, was undecided what to do with the originals. Several letters passed, and at last Carlyle wrote to a friend living in the neighbourhood, asking him to see his correspondent, and persuade him of his undoubted duty, which was at least to submit documents of such great importance to examination.

Unfortunately, the friend was absent, and by the time he returned the papers had been destroyed. They may, of course, have had no existence, but Carlyle himself was of a contrary opinion, for later on he received a heavy packet containing copies of thirty-five letters of Oliver Cromwell, written in a style apparently contemporary, and referring to incidents that no one who had not made a careful and exhaustive study of his life and times, and who was not thoroughly conversant with all the available material, would have been in the least able to reproduce.

The records were destroyed because, as the owner said, he felt that, one way or another, the manuscripts would be got from him and made public, and 'what could that amount to but a new Guy Fawkes cellar and infernal machine to explode the cathedral city where he lived, and all its coteries, and almost dissolve Nature for the time being?' Either this man was a learned forger or a singularly narrow-minded and obstinate type of destroyer whose ravages can be traced through the centuries, and whose example will never cease to be followed so long as paper remains unable to resist the assaults of the bigot and the outrages of the Goth.

That will be ever, and hence it is that in all things literary preservation is the greatest of the virtues. What part of a century's product to preserve and what to destroy is a problem, not for us, but for the century to come, and for many centuries after that. In fact, it is Time's problem, which Time alone can solve.

CHAPTER V.

SOME HUNTING-GROUNDS OF LONDON.

AT the present time there are, if the Post-Office Directory is to be believed, about 450 booksellers in London; but in this computation are included publishers, stationers, and even bookbinders—in fact, almost everyone who has anything whatever to do with books—so that the figures are by no means to be relied upon. The number of booksellers who make a speciality of second-hand volumes is very much less than 450, if we include only those who follow a single business, namely, that of buying and selling books, and very much greater if we add to the list the army of general dealers who sell books occasionally, or as an adjunct to some other occupation.

The real book-hunter does not follow the Directory, but his nose, which frequently leads him into strange places where there are no recognised booksellers, yet booksellers in plenty—a seeming paradox, which is readily explained by the fact that there are multitudes of what may, without offence, be called 'book-jobbers,' whose names are either not in the Directory at all, or appear there under some other designation.

A man may buy up a roomful of furniture, taking the books of necessity; or a houseful, and with the mass of goods and chattels perhaps hundreds of volumes which are not thought good enough to be disposed of separately, and are therefore cleared out at a nominal figure, and retailed anywhere and everywhere as circumstance and opportunity suggest. Are these dealers, brokers, and what not, booksellers? Heaven save the mark, no! not in a specific sense; but they sell books, notwithstanding, and their shops are, in very truth, recognised hunting-grounds of the Metropolis. There are literally hundreds of them, and they are to be met with, as a rule, close together, where rents are low and the footsteps of the income-tax fiend are unknown.

This is one description of bookseller, but there are several others: the man with the barrow, for instance, who works at his trade all the week, and comes out on Saturday afternoons and Sunday mornings in certain localities, to do what bartering he can with casual passers-by.

To compare these classes with the recognised booksellers, some of whom have an immense turnover, would, of course, be absurd; but they have their uses, and instances are not wanting in which mightily successful dealers have begun

Some Hunting-grounds of London 75

in this humble manner, and literally forced their way up from the pavements of the East End or the Surrey side to more pleasant places in the West. High or low, rich or poor, their shops or stalls are alike objects of extreme interest to thousands who have learned enough to know that the best books are generally the cheapest. Whatever the size of the premises they own, they contribute in their several degrees to the wants of all classes of book-men, whose delight it is to forage for themselves, and to seek that they may find. The lordly collector who pays by cheque may or may not be a book-hunter. If not, he misses much of the pleasure that accompanies the tracking down, step by step, of some coveted volume which is, perhaps, more or less easily obtainable almost at any time in exchange for plenty of money, but is rarely met with casually.

It is this tracking down, hunting, which is the true book-lover's chief delight, and, needless to say, his primary object is not to secure books of great price for a nominal sum. If it were, he would at the end of a long life have few successes to report, for the search for rarities is so thorough and systematic that hardly anything of substantial pecuniary value can run the gauntlet all the way to the shop-board or the barrow. The harvest has all been gathered long ago, and nothing is now left but gleanings in fields already raked. The book-lover eliminates as far as possible the question of value from his walks abroad, and leaves his gold at home to be expended as opportunity arises in the auction-room, where open competition holds the market in a virtual equipoise, or in the shops of recognised dealers, who hold his commissions and are always on the look-out for important works. He is aware, however, that intrinsically good books are to be met with continually in all sorts of places, and it is these that he hopes to obtain, and from these that his library is most often recruited. Between one edition of some interesting or instructive book and another there may be an immense disparity in cost, but very little textual difference, or even none at all. In some cases the cheaper volume may be the more accurate of the two, and may also contain additional matter, which renders it more important and desirable from every point of view, except a sentimental one.

It is the search for volumes of this kind, sound and honest, yet not aristocratic, that has kept the bookstalls open for 300 years and more, for, to be precise, we know that St. Paul's Churchyard and Fleet Street were, in addition to other less known localities, much frequented by bookmen as far back as the reign of Henry VIII. In these districts Cardinal Wolsey's agents kept a sharp look-out for copies of 'A Supplicacyon for the Beggars,' which Simon Fyshe, 'a zealous man for the reformation of abuses in the Church,' had boldly published and was

Some Hunting-grounds of London 77

scattering abroad in the year 1524, and which seems to have had a stealthy run for six years, for it was not until 1530 that it was openly prohibited by proclamation. Neither Fleet Street nor St. Paul's Churchyard is, however, a hunting-ground for book-men now. The former is wholly given up to newspapers and machinery, and the latter to drapers and warehousemen, and there is no room anywhere for small dealers in second-hand books.

Indeed, the whole of London has been turned topsy-turvy so far as they are concerned. New localities they abhor, and the greater part of London is new, in the sense that very many old districts and streets have been rebuilt, or entirely swept away by the march of improvement and the increasing desire for wide thoroughfares and open spaces. What place more famous once than Little Britain, which during the last twenty or thirty years has swallowed up Duck Lane— another book-hunting locality—bodily? It was here that Thomas Britton, a coal-dealer, prowled around during his spare moments, pouncing upon anything and everything that took his fancy; rejoicing especially in works of magic, witchcraft, and astrology, either printed or in manuscript. The catalogue of his library is extant, and it is clear that he was a very far-sighted and keen-scented man, and one, too, who was blessed with a taste and discrimination most rare among dealers in small coal. In Little Britain 'Paradise

Lost' went begging. The stalls must have been littered with the very first, or 1667, issue, for in that year the Earl of Dorset had a copy of it thrust under his nose and pressed upon him by a bookseller who complained most bitterly that he could not get rid of his stock. About the year 1760 the whole of the trade had vanished from Little Britain, though at the present time the once-famous thoroughfare boasts one bookseller and also one newsagent, the sole representatives of past times. As for the rest of the denizens, they follow the more prosaic occupations of builders, bootmakers, butchers, hairdressers, restaurant-keepers and publicans, the last-named being especially in evidence. In this locality, as in many others, the thirst for knowledge has been quenched, and the thirst for beer become almighty.

So, too, Moorfields was once classic ground, as also the Poultry, but both places have been dead to bookish fame this hundred years. There are now no booksellers' shops in the Poultry, though Moorfields just saves itself, for it rejoices in the presence of a music publisher and a stationer. Speaking generally, the second-hand book trade has been driven bodily out of the central and eastern parts of London, and has settled itself in the streets west of Temple Bar and Holborn Viaduct, always avoiding the Strand, which, for some reason or other, has ever been regarded as an inhospitable quarter. There are certainly booksellers' shops in this important thoroughfare, three, I believe, is the precise number, but they are hardly sufficient to invest it with the dignity and title of a 'locality.'

In contrast to this, Holborn and the streets adjoining have always been a good hunting-ground, and are so to-day. 'The Vision of Piers Plowman' was printed and sold in Ely Rents so long ago as 1550, and Snow Hill and Gray's Inn Gate were both world-wide localities, though the glory of all these places has since departed. Up to within five years ago there was a shop on the right-hand side of Gray's Inn Lane, just out of Holborn, given up chiefly to the sale of newspapers. It is shut up now, and, according to all accounts, will never be opened again, which is a pity, for it is a shop, or more probably the curtailment of much larger premises, with a notable history. Here, in 1750 or thereabouts, carried on business one Thomas Osborne, who, although ignorant to a degree, brutal in his manners, and surly beyond description, managed to build up the largest business of its kind in London, or, indeed, anywhere else. Customers ignored Tom Osborne's curses, and bought his books when they could, for sometimes, when particularly morose, he would shut himself up, like a hermit, 'with his lumber,' as a historian of the day termed the thirty whole libraries which he had amassed, and refuse to treat at all. Nevertheless, Osborne prospered exceedingly, and in the latter

years of his life was the owner of a country house
and 'dog and duck shootings,' all purchased and
kept up from the profits derived from this shop
in Gray's Inn Lane. The prices he asked were
the most he thought he had the remotest chance
of getting, and were often outrageous and extor-
tionate, though at other times very much below
what he might have obtained had he known his
business properly. He seems to have taken a
bird's-eye view of his stock, and to have appraised
the value of individual books, not by reference to
their rarity, but by means of a fractional calcula-
tion based upon the total cost—a rough-and-ready
method of trading which attracted book-buyers
from every part of London, and reconciled them
to his insolence. Though Osborne was not the
first dealer to issue a catalogue—one T. Green, of
Spring Gardens, being credited with having
revived, in 1729, this time-worn method of selling
books—he carried on a more extensive business in
this way than anyone who had preceded him, and
in addition had the supreme honour of being
knocked down by Dr. Johnson with a huge folio
which the latter wanted to buy, and he (Osborne)
refused to sell at any price. Either of these
claims to distinction would have made the fortune
of any man. It is stated by Sir John Hawkins
that the book which Dr. Johnson wielded with
such effect was the 'Biblia Græca Septuaginta,'
printed at Frankfort in 1594. The identical
volume was in the possession of Thorpe, a Cam-

Some Hunting-grounds of London 81

bridge bookseller, in 1812, but what has become of it since I do not know.

Though Osborne's shop, or what remains of it, is now closed, the neighbourhood is still as largely interested in the sale of books as ever, or perhaps even more so, for there has been an immigration from other quarters of London which improvements have converted into uncongenial ground.

The new Law Courts and their approaches stand upon the sites of Butchers' Row, Shire Lane, where Elias Ashmole lived, and countless courts and alleys beside. Clare Market has vanished within the last two or three years, and Clement's Inn, with its narrow passages and dingy chambers, has been entirely rebuilt. Even Drury Lane, sacred to the memory of an army of general dealers who, up to within a comparatively short time ago, bought books by weight, is now past praying for to all appearances, for hardly a book of any kind is to be met with from one end of this grimy thoroughfare to the other. Let us walk into Bozier's Court, which is further to the west, and we miss the shop which Lord Lytton has immortalized in 'My Novel'; in fact, the court itself is plastered all over with advertisement posters, and awaits the wreckers, for it is doomed. King William Street, Strand, was a booksellers' resort for a century and more, but the fraternity are leaving one by one, and only a very few are to be met there now. Westminster Hall, for centuries a virtual library, is shut up, and echoes spring from its stones when any casual stranger, armed with an order, is allowed to ramble through Rufus's deserted pile. In fact, wherever we stray, north, south, east, or west, we are forced to the conclusion that London has changed so utterly within the last twenty or thirty years that it is to all intents and purposes a different place.

And the booksellers appear to have changed, too, for there are no 'characters' among them, or, at any rate, very few. Every now and then you will meet with some strange mortal, who looks as though he had been transported bodily from the last century and tumbled unceremoniously into a brand new shop, with coloured glass above the portal, and fresh paint about the front; but you have hardly time to ruminate on the mutability of things under the sun and he is gone, to make way, perhaps, for a dealer in something superlatively new. An antiquary of the stamp of Francis Grose, the 'chiel' who went about taking notes, would stand aghast, then hasten to depart, could he but see the London of to-day.

It must not, however, be supposed that book-hunting as a pastime is extinct in modern Babylon. On the contrary, there are yet plenty of nooks and corners, and pestilential-looking alleys, that Death and the jerry-builder have apparently forgotten, and these places, we may be certain,.

Some Hunting-grounds of London 83

harbour many folios. As a fact, I know they do; for in my time, and to some extent even yet, I have been and am a wanderer about such places, and have, on occasion, picked up many interesting mementos there. What I merely wish to insist upon is that the older and recognised localities, which our fathers would naturally have visited a couple of decades or more ago in their search for old books, are not those which would, as a rule, afford much scope for enterprise now. We must go further afield, and not expect to find a mass of stalls huddled together in a single street, as though one locality had tapped and drained the life-blood of the rest. Circumstances have changed, and at the close of the nineteenth century booksellers have, to a great extent, ceased to be gregarious, except in Holywell Street, or, as it is more generally called, 'Booksellers' Row,' once the abode of literary hacks and bailiff-haunted debtors, which even yet has an old-world look with its overhanging houses and narrow roadway. Here there certainly is a long double procession of bookshops, many open to the street, every one of them crammed from floor to ceiling with great piles of lore.

And Holywell Street, be it said, is such historic and classic ground, that it is threatened every day by the improver, who longs to lay its north side open to the Strand, and will, we may be sure, effect his purpose in the end. It was here that Lord Macaulay used to take his walks abroad in

6—2

search of books. As a rule he began and ended there; for a whole day's pilgrimage would not suffice to unearth more than a fractional part of the immense store of volumes that the labour of years had accumulated, and which was continually being decimated and renewed. In his day there were more books to be seen and handled there than now, for some of the shops have since been devoted to other trades. In Holywell Street John Payne Collier was as well known as his own 'History of English Dramatic Poetry,' which, nearly sixty years ago, littered the stalls, doubtless to his great disgust, seeing that to be in evidence there to any extent was then, as now, proof positive that the 'remainder-man' had been at work, to the bane of the author and publisher alike. Mr. W. Roberts, in his charming 'Book-hunter in London,' narrates that Collier once picked up in Holywell Street for the merest trifle a copy of John Hughes's 'Calypso and Telemachus,' an opera in three acts, first published in 1712, which contained thirty-eight unpublished couplets in the handwriting of Pope. Halliwell-Phillipps was also an inveterate rambler up and down this thoroughfare, and several of his Shakespearean quartos came from there in days when these small but almost priceless volumes were not so widely and persistently sought for as they are now. In fact, we have it in his own words that when he first began to collect anything and everything that related in whatever degree

Some Hunting-grounds of London 85

to the great dramatist, these early quartos were frequently to be met with at prices which, comparatively speaking, sound simply ludicrous in our ears. Should anyone rescue a copy now from some forgotten lumber-room, the fact is heralded by the press, and accounted most extraordinary, as indeed it is; for everyone, the world over, is on the look-out for rarities such as these. Though Holywell Street yet stands, and does a thriving trade among the bookish, let not anyone think that much is to be got for nothing there. On the contrary, the dealers who inhabit it are better versed than most people in the importance of each and every book they part with or throw into the boxes which receive the outcasts of literature. There are, however, good and valuable books by the thousand to be met with by anyone who does not object to pay a fair and reasonable price for them. To this extent, and in this particular, is Booksellers' Row the queen of London streets. From these remarks I except, of course, the extremely important shops of the West-End dealers into which correspondence flows from every part of the world.

This chapter is devoted to the 'Hunting-grounds' of London, and I deny that a collector who gives a standing order either verbally or by letter to a bookseller for some work he particularly wants is a book-hunter at all, at least so far as that particular transaction is concerned. To my mind Nimrod must handle his own bow and not entrust it to a deputy, even though he might by the rules of the chase be absolutely entitled to the quarry which the skill of the latter had brought down. Let him go where he will, East or West, the point of the compass makes no matter, he is a hunter only when he prosecutes his own inquiries and carries out in person all his arrangements. So we will avoid the great firms of booksellers, although it may be taken for granted that almost any scarce work could be procured sooner or later from them, and go off on a chase in which we shall never, in all human probability, meet with any great prize, and may have to be satisfied with a little, that little, however, being much from many points of view.

At the present day books of all sorts are to be met with in great profusion in Farringdon Street. Every Saturday morning throughout the year light hand-carts to the number, perhaps, of thirty or forty, stand in a long line against the curb, and each is packed with works of all kinds. I am bound to admit that obsolete school-books and forgotten sermons constitute the great majority of these waifs and strays, but there is always a wide choice of useful books to be got for purely nominal sums, and occasionally one that is rare and valuable. Personally I never met with a really scarce book in Farringdon Street, but three years ago—and I mention this at the risk of being charged with travelling from the subject—I bought there the undoubtedly original study by

Some Hunting-grounds of London 87

Sir Joshua Reynolds for the portrait of the Right Honourable George Seymour Conway, afterwards Lord George Seymour Conway. The portrait was painted in 1770, and engraved in mezzotint by Edward Fisher the year following. The study is in oils, on thick paper of about twelve inches in height, and is so remarkable as a work of art, that it is a wonder it could have escaped recognition for an hour, instead, as was the fact, for a whole morning.

Should Farringdon Street prove unpropitious, Sunday morning in any week will see Lambeth Marshes and the New Cut, both on the Surrey side, crowded with barrows, and the same remark applies to the streets about the Elephant and Castle on Saturday evenings when the weather is fine. Generally speaking, the peripatetic bookseller is only to be met with on the first and last days of the week, but that he does manage to turn over a considerable part of his stock in the short time available is not to be doubted. He may not change—many of these men have haunted the same spot for years, and have their recognised stands—but his stock is, in one sense, ever new. A few months ago I saw in the Whitechapel Road a hand-cart full of small vellum-bound volumes, which proved to be Greek and Latin classics, printed in Paris a couple of centuries ago. The covers were remarkably fresh and clean, and somebody or other, or rather a succession of owners, must have taken the greatest care of these little books, which had thus ignobly fallen into the gutter at last. Next week at the same hour, they had all gone, having been disposed of to the more learned inhabitants of Bethnal Green at 2d. apiece.

If, however, wandering about the East End of London is not to the taste of the picker-up of unconsidered trifles, there is still the more primitive kind of shops to be visited. Great Turnstile still boasts a bookseller or two, and it was here, it will be remembered, that John Bagford, many years ago, divided his attention between making boots and shoes and ripping out the title-pages of the books that fell into his sacrilegious hands. He failed as a cobbler, but succeeded in amassing the most disreputable collection of titles that has ever been got together. The arch-Vandal failed in everything but his Vandalism, and surely any success is better than none at all. It is said of him that he searched all his life for one of Caxton's impossible title-pages, and died of disappointment, a story which is probably a gross libel on his accomplishments, for Bagford was not by any means an uneducated man.

Then, Little Turnstile hard by is worth a casual visit, and there are many shops in the streets extending east and west of St. Martin's Lane where books are to be bought in almost any number. The newly-built Charing Cross Road appears to be under a cloud; in fact, at

Some Hunting-grounds of London 89

this point we must turn back again, and make direct for Holborn, Bury Street, and the neighbourhood of Red Lion Square and Queen Square.

In Red Lion Passage there are several of the quaintest shops imaginable, one of them kept by a dealer who appears to have a mania for the very largest folios, though I notice that of late he has somewhat fallen away from his traditional custom in this respect. The books stand on their sides on the floor in columns of about six feet high; they are piled on and under the counter, and are seen peeping out of the black darkness of a room beyond. Petrarch would have avoided this shop lest history should repeat itself, and a folio break, not his leg merely this time, but his neck.

On the other side of the Passage is another temple of gloom and mystery, for it must be observed that the neighbourhood of Red Lion Square is generally in semi-darkness all the year round, except in the winter, and then it is frequently impossible to see at all when once the streets are left. The proprietors of this shop issue a periodical catalogue, which can be taken from a box at the door, and it may safely be said that there is no catalogue issued in London by anyone which is better worth glancing over than this, notwithstanding an occasional misprint or two. The books are, generally speaking, of such an unusual and out-of-the-way kind that one cannot help wondering where they all come from. For

8vo., 1732,' must be a remarkable volume, and the ' Wuremberg Chronicle, folio, numerous woodcuts, 1493,' equally curious. Then there is ' Peasson on the Creed,' 'Jewels, ——, Works, folio, 1611,' ' Locke, Humane Understanding, folio, 1706,' 'Staunton : Shakispear,' and so on *ad infinitum*. Throughout the prices are moderate, extremely moderate; that, at any rate, is a fact worthy of distinct recognition, and some of the books, too, are anything but easy to procure, as witness Chaucer's Works, folio, 1602, which is priced at £1 10s., Grafton's Chronicle, folio, 1569, £1 5s., Swan's ' Speculum Mundi,' 4to., 1670, 3s., and many others. Dark though this shop may be to gaze upon, I regard it as a typical bookman's paradise.

Paternoster Row, further east still, is now, of course, the headquarters of the publishers, though several second-hand booksellers still linger there. Before the Great Fire reduced the whole district to ashes they had it all their own way, and when the Row was rebuilt they flocked there once more, to be gradually elbowed out by giant houses which sell books wholesale. There is one shop in this thoroughfare so completely wedged up with books that it is a somewhat difficult matter to enter in at the door. Nobody who is not in the daily habit of passing by could avoid stopping to glance at the rows of volumes which the proprietor has reared up against a wall round the corner that leads into St. Paul's Churchyard, for he has decorated them with innumerable strips of paper writ large with pieces of advice on things in general, quotations from classical writers, the Bible and the Koran, which, though they have for the most part nothing whatever to do with the sale of books of any kind, attract by reason of their quaintness and the strangeness of their being.

And so we might go wandering for ever about New London, passing on every side the shadows of the old, but seeing little of the substance. Bookmen of the true stamp are antiquaries, to whom novelty is abhorrent. The pleasantest places are to them those which time has consecrated with a gentle touch, and which reflect all their imaginings, even as they echo their footsteps. These are departing under the mandate of an inexorable law, and we go with them.

CHAPTER VI.

VAGARIES OF BOOK-HUNTERS.

TEN or fifteen years ago it was quite usual to meet with collections of title-pages formed by followers of the immortal Bagford. These were to be seen quoted in booksellers' catalogues and displayed in the auction rooms, and were commonly disposed of for small sums of money—small, that is to say, in comparison with what would have been realized for the books themselves had they been allowed to remain in that state of life to which the author and others had called them. Of late, collections of title-pages have not been very much in evidence anywhere, for it is universally felt that there is little or no romance surrounding the slaughter even of folios, to say nothing of smaller-sized victims, and for that reason these scrappy collections are huddled out of sight like family skeletons. The book-hunter of the present day has his foibles, it is true, but he has learned by experience and from the expostulatory remarks of others that wild freaks are completely out of place in a library, and so it

Vagaries of Book-hunters 93

has come to pass that books are treated in a different way from what they were only a couple of decades ago, and no one who has the smallest respect either for himself or his vocation would now either care or dare to form a collection of title-pages. Should he happen to own one either by purchase or under circumstances beyond his control, he will produce it, if at all, with apologies and sighs. It is abundantly manifest that the wicked man hath turned away from much of his wickedness.

The reason of this tremendous transformation must be put down to the credit of a rule which, though formulated and preached at one time by the élite only, has been insisted upon with such pertinacity that it has gradually become diffused throughout the whole world of collectors, no matter to what objects of interest they may direct their attention. This rule is, that taste and the pocket alike demand that be a book good, bad, or indifferent in its externals, it shall, nevertheless, be left untouched by its owner, who is but its temporary custodian, and a trustee for others who shall come after him. To rip out the title-page, no matter with what object, is an outrage on decency which, it is pleasant to find, is now appraised at its proper pitch of enormity. If the stamp-collector rejoice in the possession of a specimen with 'original gum,' and rate its interest and value higher on that account, shall the book-collector, who is the oldest, the most learned, and the most aristocratic of all collectors, give place in the matter of common-sense and discretion to the product of a frivolous age ? Shall he cut initial letters from missals and other manuscripts, and insult the shades of Füst and Schoiffer by making a senseless collection of colophons ? These things were in vogue at one time, but are now frowned down even by the most ignorant of mortals, since, to put the matter on no higher ground, the money value of old books has considerably increased of late years to his certain knowledge, and he believes that anything with curious type, the f's made so—*f*, and villainous prints scattered about the text, must *ex necessitate rei* be worth its weight in gold, and perhaps more. What a contrast is this little false, but preventative, store of knowledge to the crass stupidity of the early years of the present century, as exemplified in the persons of the Bishops, Canons, and Chaplains of Lincoln Cathedral, who permitted the choir-boys to collect illuminated initials, and with that object to cut up with their pen-knives scores of vellum manuscripts. A good many of the Caxtons from this same Cathedral were purchased by Dibdin for the Althorp collection, and will be found catalogued in 'A Lincolne Nosegaye.' The Dean and Chapter, knowing little about books, and caring less, had disposed of them all for a 'consideration,' and thus without thought stripped themselves of their choicest possessions next to the Cathedral itself.

Of a truth, books have only recently come to be regarded as possessing a sentimental value altogether distinct from considerations of utility, and it is only within the compass of a comparatively few years that collectors have sprung up from the very stones to cry aloud, and to protest against such wanton acts of mutilation or destruction as the records of past days almost choke themselves in the echoing of. Only a little while ago 'Grangerizing' was the favourite pastime of thousands of persons of elegant leisure, as Griswold called the lazy dullards of his generation, and what this involved would be whispered in corners but for the fact that it was for 200 years unblushingly shouted in the open day.

During all that period the teachings of the genuine bibliophiles had so passed from deed and truth into mere monotony of unbelieved phrase that no English was literal enough to convert the persons who went about seeking material, at vast expense, wherewith to extra-illustrate some inane book of polemics or proverbs.

Nicholas Ferrar, who kept the 'Protestant Nunnery' at Little Gidding, in Huntingdonshire, was, I believe, the inventor of a system which was not fully developed until the publication of Granger's 'Biographical History of England,' but which is, nevertheless, directly or indirectly responsible for the condition of most of the imperfect volumes which are met with at every turn.

The story of Nicholas Ferrar, assuming it to be true, which there is little reason to doubt, makes it clear that King Charles I. was as bad as or worse than anybody in this matter, for, had he not affected to admire the handiwork of this first and chief of sinners, the baneful practice of mutilating books for the sake of their illustrations, title-pages, or frontispieces, might never have become an aristocratic amusement, sanctified by tradition, and ennobled far beyond its deserts by kingly patronage. The Concordance which Ferrar showed the King escaped the wrath of the fanatic Hugh Peters and his crew, and, after many vicissitudes, is now safely lodged in the British Museum, a warning to all who may at any time seek to revive a practice which would, in these days of emulation and competition, burn with a white heat.

In Wordsworth's 'Ecclesiastical Biography' the story of Nicholas Ferrar is set out at length. There is no need to enter into minute details, as the tale has since become stereotyped, and is found reproduced in a dozen different places at least. Shortly, it appears that in June, 1634, King Charles I. was staying with the Earl of Westmorland at Apethorpe, and from thence sent one of his gentlemen to the home of Nicholas Ferrar, hard by, to 'intreat' a sight of a Concordance which he had heard had recently been completed. When Ferrar was on the Continent some time previously, he had bought up a great number of prints by the best masters, illustrative of historical passages of the Old and New Testaments, and these he afterwards used for ornamenting various compilations of the Scriptures, among them a 'full harmony or concordance of the four Evangelists, adorned with many beautiful pictures, which required more than a year for the composition, and was divided into 150 heads or chapters.'

This was the Concordance that King Charles was so anxious to look at, and which, indeed, he admired so much that he never rested until he had obtained one like it for his own library. Both books are now in the British Museum, the original having been acquired about three years ago, and the one in the King's Library from George II., who had inherited the royal collection of books and manuscripts.

From the point of view of Nicholas Ferrar, there was certainly no harm in this process of extra-illustrating. There is no reason to believe that he had gone about tearing out plates from books, or done anything else which in any respect, save one, could be regarded as objectionable in the slightest degree. There was, and is, however, one objection to his procedure, namely, the very bad example he set to unscrupulous people who, in after years, rose up in their thousands and commenced to rip and tear with diabolical enterprise. These were the days of Granger's 'Biographical History of England'—hence the verb to Grangerize—when people went about searching for portraits of celebrities mentioned in the text to paste between the leaves in their proper places. If Granger incidentally mentioned that someone had been conveyed to the Tower, and subsequently had the good fortune to escape out of a certain window, books would be ransacked and mutilated to provide illustrations of (1) the Tower of London from the N., S., E. or W., as the case might be; (2) portrait of the prisoner; (3) view of the window from which he let himself down; and finally, if, *Laus Deo*, a letter in his handwriting or a section of the rope which had made his escape possible could only be unearthed, great was the joy in the camp of the Philistine.

This mania for Grangerizing grew till it assumed enormous proportions. One enthusiast tried to illustrate Rees' 'Cyclopædia,' but died before he had accomplished very much in comparison with what remained to be done. Mr. Crowle's copy of Pennant's 'History of London' cost that gentleman £7,000 from first to last, and there is a book of this kind in the Bodleian which has engulfed nearly double that amount. It consists of Clarendon's 'History of the Rebellion,' swollen to sixty-seven large volumes, representing forty years of intense application. The vagaries of a whole army of book-collectors are reflected from every page of works such as these, for a man must necessarily be a book-collector first, and a Grangerizer after, else would material fail him. Happily for the peace of books, the mania for extra-illustrating has practically died out. The expense is too great, life too short, the knowledge and taste—of a kind—too laborious to acquire, to endow this pastime with a permanent and stable interest.

And yet there is another vagary, eccentricity, freak, or what you will, which, for cool, deliberate folly, has never been equalled even among Ferrar's admirers. The fun in this case consists in wilfully destroying a certain number of scarce and valuable books in order to heighten the importance and value of the survivors. Three or four collectors whose tastes are similar—that is to say, who accumulate works by the same author—will take stock of their belongings. Thanks to the Grangerizers, a portrait will perhaps be missing from one volume, and a plate from another; some disciple of an ancient Goth may have removed a title-page or two; one copy may be fairer to look upon than another; a leaf or two may be injured which in another copy, imperfect perhaps in other respects, may be above suspicion. Our collectors have duplicates, for they have been striving all their lives to prevent anyone else from obtaining any copy, good, bad, or indifferent, of the scarcest works of the author or authors they think they honour by their notice. They make a 'pool' of all the volumes which are not immaculate; complete or perfect as many of them as possible, apportion them, and destroy the remainder. They will burn a work which is perfect, provided each has a copy in better condition, and this is to prevent you or me, or anyone else, from sharing in their sacrilegious joy. When we reflect that, from the nature of things, it is only the scarcest books that can be so treated with effect, we shall begin to realize the sinister importance of the act. Practices such as these are the product of the present age; they are not common, far from it, but they are not unusual. And yet the perpetrators mean no harm, for, as they would very truly say, if their practices were generally known and complaint were made, ' You can, if you like, read So-and-so without the least difficulty, for his works have been reprinted many times, and it is not either essential or advisable that the very scarcest edition of all should be in your hands.' There is in this argument a little logical force, but no decency for anyone to dissect.

Bookmen of the present day, or at least those among them who aspire to the highest seats in the collectors' Pantheon, are invariably bound by rule, and it is this hard and fast bondage that makes them do things which, if left to themselves, they would probably be the first to deprecate. To accumulate any considerable number of really scarce books is the labour of a lifetime, and to obtain immaculate copies necessitates not merely the possession of plenty of money, but a very great deal of energy, discrimination, and tact.

Vagaries of Book-hunters 101

The old school of general lovers is dying out. People now very seldom buy up whole libraries, or send out colossal orders to gratify a mere love of possession. They work by the book of arithmetic, cautiously, slowly, and with one main object ever in view. In this they are right, but in this also they fail, a paradox which is no paradox at all when it is remembered that book-hunters are of many kinds and of varying degrees of intelligence.

For instance, though there is undoubtedly something unique and strange about the very appearance of a library of extremely diminutive books, the collector of works of this kind is 'cabin'd, cribb'd, confin'd,' within the compass of about two square inches at the most, and probably does not expect to derive either instruction or amusement from their pages when he has succeeded in reading them with the aid of a microscope. His rule is inflexible. Shakespeare in folio must give place to 'The Mite'; 'The English Bijou Almanac' for 1837 is, in his eyes, one of the choicest of all volumes. Here literature and the rule are in conflict, and books become bric-à-brac, as they must do when any rule is too rigidly applied to them. Yet there are many collectors of small books both here and abroad, and prices rule inordinately high in consequence.

Very probably 'The Mite' is the smallest book printed from movable type in the world. Its size is only ⅜ in. by ¾ in., and it would certainly be an exceedingly difficult matter to reduce this measurement. If anybody could do so, it would be M. Salomon of Paris, who has long been a collector of these microscopical curiosities, or the trustees of the British Museum, who have a box full of them. In 1781 a little book called the 'Alarm Almanac' made its appearance in Paris, and though printed with movable type and not engraved, like nearly all these little works are, measured only 19 millimètres by 14. There are very nearly 25½ millimètres to the inch, and this specimen consequently runs 'The Mite' very close indeed. The 'English Bijou Almanac' for 1837, however, completely eclipses both, but unfortunately it is engraved and not printed from type. This book measures ¾ in. in height, ½ in. wide, and ⅛ in. in thickness. The authoress was 'L.E.L.,' Letitia Elizabeth Landon, an almost forgotten poetess, whose sad marriage and untimely death are known to only a few students of Victorian literature. Some of her poems were printed in the 'Bijou' for the first and only time, so that this tiny volume is of some literary importance. Its title is so minute that a magnifying glass is necessary to read it. Its thirty-seven leaves are devoted, *inter alia*, to several pages of music and some portraits, including one of James Fenimore Cooper, the novelist. Even small books have a history and an importance of their own, but to collect them to the exclusion

Vagaries of Book-hunters 103

of every other book is surely a pronounced 'vagary.'

M. Salomon has more than 200 specimens, but then he does not absolutely confine his attention to midgets. I never knew nor heard of more than one collector who was so infatuated as to do so, and he had forty-five volumes of the kind, all different, in which he took such extreme delight that he was ever on the look out for more.

Another collector with whom I am personally acquainted has read this chapter through at my express request, and consequently cannot reasonably say that I have endeavoured to question the soundness of his discretion behind his back. He accumulates books with a history. If a book has no history, he will have none of it. In his library are many volumes which I must confess I have a great regard for, but which I know can never be mine, for each is unique, and the whole collection is destined for a public museum in the end.

He has a book bound in what looks like dry and hard parchment, warped with damp, and stained here and there with reddish brown. It is a copy of Johnson's 'Lives and Adventures of the most Famous Highwaymen, Murderers, and Street Robbers, etc.,' printed in folio in 1736, a scarce book at any time, but under existing circumstances past praying for. The parchment is human cuticle, stripped from the back of a criminal who had swung at Tyburn for a series of atrocious butcheries, which are chronicled with considerable minuteness in the pages of the 'Newgate Calendar.' When the corpse was cut down it was, according to the custom then prevailing, carted 'home,' and exhibited to gaping crowds at so much a head, and finally sold to the surgeons. From them a prior owner of this delightful volume obtained the skin, which, when tanned, formed an appropriate and never-to-be-forgotten binding, to all appearances sweating great smears of blood. It is only the damp, of course, or perhaps some defect in the curing process, which is responsible for these blemishes; but they seem to cry for vengeance, still greater and greater vengeance, against an inhuman wretch long since departed more or less in peace.

This is the only gruesome thing in the library, and I know as a fact that it excites more interest than all the rest of the books put together, though many, not to say most, of them are distinctly worthy of the closest attention. One volume belonged to Charles Lamb, who has made a perfect wreck of it, and half a dozen or more have the signature of 'Will Shakespere' scribbled in an Elizabethan hand on the title-pages, and in all sorts of places. These were once among the choicest possessions of Samuel Ireland, of Norfolk Street, Strand, the father of William Henry Ireland, a liar and a solicitor's clerk, who, as all the world knows, was for a time, and in very truth, mistaken for the great dramatist himself.

Vagaries of Book-hunters 105

Then there are books with inscriptions, undoubtedly genuine, of Bradshaw the regicide, Algernon Sidney, and many other persons of the highest political eminence in their day; books, too, which have belonged to Young the poet—distinguishable at a glance by the multitude of turned-down leaves—and the unfortunate Louis XVI.

This library is, of its kind, perhaps as important as any that has ever been formed, and yet it only numbers some 250 volumes, so supremely difficult is it, as a rule, to trace the possession even of books for more than a generation or two. Great men have ever been chary of their names, or at least it would seem so from the number of unimportant signatures and inscriptions we meet with day by day.

A long and very interesting chapter might be written on 'Inscriptions in Books,' and it must be confessed that a really important signature or comment adds so very appreciably to the sentimental value of the volume in which it is found, that it is not surprising that Oliver Wendell Holmes conjured up a pleasant train of reflection, in his inimitable style, based upon the name of a former owner of his own copy of the 'Colloquies of Erasmus,' which, by the way, my friend is extremely anxious to possess himself of, but will probably never obtain. In this instance the personality of the 'Autocrat of the Breakfast-Table' obscures all else, and gives the book a distinct history of its own—a history that invests it with an importance and value it could never claim of itself. To find out all we can about the former owners of books which we ourselves take pleasure in is no frivolous task, and the pity is that our opportunities for doing so are limited. The book-plate has very nearly put an end to owner's autographs, and being easy to remove, affords little or no guarantee of ownership. And book-plates have been in use in this country for more than 200 years.

No doubt everyone who has anything to do with books, whether as writer, producer, or collector, can call to mind the eccentricities of his neighbours with regard to them. I call it extremely eccentric conduct on the part of any man to persist in collecting odd volumes, and to studiously ignore complete sets. Yet I knew an old gentleman—now dead, and his books littering the stalls of Farringdon Street and elsewhere—who did this, year after year, and for many years, with the inevitable result. He was fond of literature, and the pleasure he derived in reading was part and parcel of his existence.

It was an axiom with him, however, that anything which is worth having, and any knowledge worth acquiring, must be laboriously worked for; and he would instance numerous authorities who have taught this truth by example as well as by precept. He would say, 'If I go out and buy a Bible for £500, because it is old and scarce, do you think I shall derive as much benefit and solace from its pages as if I had invested a trifle with the fixed determination to read what I had acquired and to follow its teachings ?'

' No, certainly not,' is the obvious and truthful reply to that ; but this would appear to be different from buying one volume of, say, Pope's works when there ought to be twenty, and trusting to enterprise not unmingled with luck to discover the remaining nineteen. To this, however, he would not agree, and, to do him justice, he did not preach one thing and perform another. His theory was that, if the perusal of an odd volume leads the reader to long for the possession of its fellows, it is better that he should search for them until he finds them, than that he should have them to his hand, as it were, ready made.

Carlyle intimated that a man had far better study the title-page of any book worth the trouble of looking at than read the whole text with a vacant mind, and no doubt he was right, though this, too, seems to be an entirely distinct matter from the general principle that nothing can be learned without a maximum of inconvenience. Such a conclusion is rather a straining of the position insisted upon by Nero's tutor, that no one should collect more books than he can read, and that a multitude of books only distracts the mind. Therefore was it that Francis Bissari in the year 1750 designed a plate, which he pasted in the few volumes he possessed, and which consequently is now extremely scarce. ' Ex - Libris civis Francisci

Bissari,' he says, 'Distrahit animum librorum multitudo, itaque cum legere non possis quantum habueris, sat est habere quantum legas. Seneca. Ep. 2.'

Still, as I have intimated, the old gentleman had his way and his day, and when he died his books were all despatched to the auction rooms. It took three men more than a week to pack them in boxes. There were books under every bed in the house, and every nook and cranny was full of them. There were, altogether, many thousands of volumes, and nearly all were odd. If a series were found to be complete, as sometimes happened, it was sure to be made up of volumes belonging to different editions, and, naturally enough, in different bindings. The auctioneers did what they could, and sold the vast majority in 'parcels' for a mere song, which in truth was all they were worth.

This peculiar form of book-collecting, though apparently strange, is, and always has been, very usual, for the vast majority of readers are poor. One volume will cost less, proportionately, than the complete set of which it forms part; and, moreover, we are again face to face with the argument that it is better to master the contents of one volume than to have a mere superficial knowledge of a dozen or more. The only thing is that, as the world wags at present, the advice is erratic, and the system of buying books in sections one that cannot be recommended. If we could be sure of a hundred years of life, then things might be different. *Sed Ars longa, vita brevis est.*

And so it happens that the vagaries of book-hunters are often passing strange. Some, like Sir Thomas Phillipps, will buy largely, and never even open the cases in which they arrive. Others will hide them in all sorts of out-of-the-way places, while others again will cut them to pieces, or in some other way destroy them utterly. It is the most usual thing, for me, at any rate, and therefore presumably for others who are known to write about books, or to give the reports of the auction-rooms, to receive a bundle of title-pages as samples of the volumes to which they belong, with a request for information as to how they ought to be bound, and what they are worth. Some collectors—real *bonâ-fide* collectors these— start life with strong opinions as to the usefulness of books, and, after the manner of Grolier, though without his discretion, open their doors to all sorts and conditions of men, only to close them later with a firm resolve that, come what come may, they will never again allow any friend whomsoever even to gaze upon their store. Some, too, are so deeply immersed in their all-absorbing hobby that they have no clear conception of the difference between *meum* and *tuum*. Estimable in every respect but one, and scrupulously honest to a degree in all matters of daily intercourse, they yet fail in this one supreme trial. And yet they are absolved; for these unfortunates are not thieves.

but eccentrics, who would no more think of selling the objects they have mistaken for their own, than they would of getting wealth by false pretences. Pope Innocent X., when still Monsignor Pamphilio, was found in the possession of a book he could not satisfactorily account for, and the ludicrous part of the matter was that Du Moustier, who claimed that it had been abstracted from his library, was subsequently proved to have stolen it himself. Then, again, Catherine de Medici sequestered the entire library of Marshal Strozzi, and on complaint promised to pay for it by instalments, which, of course, she never did. Hearne hints more than once that Sir Thomas Bodley was eccentric, and when Moore, Bishop of Ely, and father of English Black-Letter Collectors, went to dine with a bibliophile, as was his wont, the latter would, if he were wise, spend the morning in removing out of sight, and, therefore, out of temptation's way, the choicest of his possessions. But the king of all these suspicious characters was Libri, who, as Inspector-General of French Libraries, under Louis Philippe, presented himself, from first to last, with books of the value of more than £20,000, among them a fine MS. of the Pentateuch, which he sold to the late Lord Ashburnham on condition that it was not to be published for twenty years. In 1868 the time expired, and then the matter was traced home, to his memory's shame.

This conduct of Libri in selling what did not

belong to him puts him, indeed, on a level, in point of turpitude, with the young divinity student of Chicago commonly called 'The Champion Biblioklept of America.' In vastness of conception the latter was a mere tyro, for he only stole a few hundred books of small value from the Chicago Public Library. The motive of both men was, however, the same, and it was that which, according to some consciences, made them thieves. After all, it is this motive that must be primarily considered in all ethical questions such as those which underlie, to some extent at least, the vagaries of every book-hunter who ever was born to hunger and thirst for Caxton's types, and paper white as snow, bound in a dream by the Gascon's magic touch.

CHAPTER VII.

HOW FASHION LIVES.

THE dim haze which, in the imagination of the populace, once floated above the head of every hungry book-man, was never in those days identified with a mass of tangled, waving hair, which, aureola-like, 'girt his occiput about,' for he was no minor poet, with pale, eager face and love-locks everywhere, but a man, with a rugged front such as Ben Jonson wore, and a heart that beat within. The haze in which he moved was from the dust of old-world tomes; it settled on his coat, and, had he worn a bob-wig, it would have settled on that also, but, since wigs had escaped the fashion of fifty years before, it merely clung to his hair instead, and powdered it gray before its time. Half a century ago the England which for the most part was free from the shriek of the railway-whistle and the rumble of traffic harboured such men as these in their hundreds. They came from the last century, and the further their pilgrimage in this the more they haunted the rustic element in which they

How Fashion Lives

moved. They were, in their way, magicians, wearing the consecrated pentacles of Agrippa, 'that man of parts, who dived into the secrets of all arts, that second Solomon, the mighty Hee, that try'de them all, and found them Vanity.'

Naturally enough, when one of these old-time bookworms left his seclusion to mix with the whirl and throng of the London thoroughfares, he was swallowed up, as though he had never been, in a huge vortex of unappreciative apathy, for the man in the street never has time to dream, and such books as he affects are ledgers. But he might have strayed into some square which the tide, ebbing westward, had left desolate, and met his counterpart sitting, as he himself did when at home, in the midst of vellum-bound classics far into the night. Indeed, when he came to London, which was but seldom, it would be to visit another bookworm, just as the stage-doorkeeper of the present day spends his evening off at the entrance to another theatre, because he cannot get away, even in spirit, from his life's work and enterprise. Were we to look for these old book-men now, we should look in vain, for the century is fast drawing to its close, and a younger generation has occupied their seats.

The transition from the old to the new in the matter of books and all that pertains to them, has been very gradual. It commenced about fifty years ago, or a little earlier, and was due, perhaps, to the spirit of unrest fostered by an improved and quicker system of communication in a country of very small area, absolutely incapable of enlargement. We see a mighty change in everything external, and it is not surprising that our social habits should have experienced a revolution. Round goes the wheel, slowly and persistently, and we go with it, though daily custom and daily experience has a tendency to mask its motion. One day, sooner or later, we start up and look for the familiar landmarks. They are gone. New ones, not at all familiar, but still recognisable, have taken their place, and then we know that time has slipped away while we were dreaming, and that nothing can possibly be done but to take the future by the forelock, and to rush on for a brief space with the rest.

And so it is with books, and ever has been. Fifty years and more ago, time waited upon them and stood still; now they are carried along unceasingly, and have no rest. Every year the speed increases. Old companions of the shelf are whirled into space and parted for ever; the very men who buy them are changed in their aspirations, their tastes, and their desires, and in a very short time they will change again, and yet again. They are swayed and driven by Fashion, and this is how Fashion lives.

There was something about the dry-as-dust bookworm which, however consonant with antiquated modes of thought and action, was never-

How Fashion Lives 115

theless felt to be utterly unsuitable to changed conditions. Men must and will read, and to accumulate is equally natural. A life of easy contentment engenders one mode of thought, a life of enterprise another; and the transition from the narrow limits of a prison-bound study to the open air is precisely what might have been expected to occur.

Men there were, as I have said, in plenty, who refused to quit the time-honoured traditions of their race; but on every side of them were being born lighter spirits, to whom colossal and intricate volumes were as heavy as lead. We see the changed nature of their tastes in the craving for art, and the outcome of it in scores and hundreds of miscellanies which began to be published about the year 1830, and held imperial sway on drawing-room tables for ten years or more.

Fisher's 'Scrap-Book,' and numerous other artistically got up volumes full of excerpts and elegant extracts, illustrated by some of the first engravers of the time, were extremely fashionable in those days, and for light and casual reading very probably supplied all that was necessary. The poets, from the Earl of Surrey onward, were served up in dainty *plats*, and the best prose authors were disembowelled with remarkable skill. The ingenious Martin Tupper, observing this transformation scene, brought joy into many households by laying down, in the form of explicit statements, matters of theological controversy which had in their day fed the Smithfield fires till they roared and blazed like those of Moloch.

These books were for the cultured, to whom the random books of Pierce Egan and William Combe were positively distasteful, and who, having neither the time nor the inclination to bury themselves deeply in classic lore, eagerly welcomed anything which appealed to their better selves and, at the same time, did not too severely tax their brains. The very style and nature of the books which were published at this period show as conclusively as anything can do the great change which was gradually creeping over the public mind.

Smollett and Swift were becoming coarse, and Hogarth, in his realm of art, was already much worse. Mrs. Radcliffe and the Rev. Mr. Maturin stalked like a couple of terrifying ghosts hung about with chains, wailing their lost home. They invariably spoke of haunted caverns, and the wind rumbling itself to sleep in the recesses of ruined chimneys. Their novels were the delight of these same dry-as-dusts, to whom the new age had said farewell, but who, in their impenetrable fastnesses, still revelled, though in numbers yearly decreasing, in 'The Raven,' with its soul-quaking refrain, in the 'Castle of Otranto,' and 'The Bravo of Venice.' Things of graver mood they could not find had they searched the entire catalogue of English literature, from the metrical poems of Cædmon, chanted to the winds of Whitby, down to the newest poem or novel.

The new school called the old 'unhealthy,' that being a not inapt adjective with which to express the absence of brightness and *chic*, qualities which came, as everything else comes, when called for, and which were embodied to a nicety in ' Sketches by " Boz,"' 'The Pickwick Papers,' and later on in 'The Yellowplush Correspondence,' and 'The Paris Sketch-Book.' The new poetry was represented by Tennyson, Browning, Longfellow, and many more, and essays of better, or, at any rate, more taking, style than those of the Rev. Vicessimus Knox, were published every day, and what is more to the point, extensively read and hoarded.

Collections which had their beginnings in materials such as these authors afforded were, and necessarily must be, totally different in every possible way from those of the prior century; this we find to be the case on looking at the catalogues of sales by auction which were issued under the new régime. Fashion had indeed changed, and at this particular period Hakluyt and Coryat, to say nothing of curious authors like Brathwaite and Seller, were comparatively neglected. They have recovered themselves since, because a revulsion of feeling has taken place in their favour, and many of the old books which were of immense importance sixty or seventy years ago are, after suffering a period of neglect, once more in vogue, and can hardly be met with when sought after, so great is the demand for them. That is the case now, but there is a wide intervening period which needs to be analyzed.

In my opinion, Dickens among novelists, and Tennyson among poets, had the greatest amount of influence upon modern collectors as a body. The former was the more powerful at first, since he had the good fortune to meet with extremely talented artists like George Cruikshank, Hablot Browne, Seymour and Leech, to illustrate his works. Cruikshank was fresh from the glories of 'Life in London,' and 'The Life of Napoleon,' which had between them carried his name far and wide, and Browne hit off the meaning of the author in such a marvellous way, that he may almost be said to have discovered him. Seymour's opportunities were few, as his seven etchings for the 'Pickwick Papers' were all he ever accomplished for Dickens; but these were, in their way, masterly, and no doubt contributed greatly to the success of the earlier parts in which they appeared.

Slowly but surely the collectors began to turn their thoughts to the new author and the artists who were assisting him, and to accumulate the numbers in which it was the fashion to issue illustrated novels at that time. We often see them now, almost as clean and fresh as when they were first published, showing conclusively that every care has been bestowed upon them. In later days, up to within a year or two in fact, there was a great rush for any books or parts by popular authors containing first-rate illustrations. There is a demand for them now, but only when their condition is immaculate, for fashion has recently changed in a marked degree, owing, perhaps, to the number of rich collectors, who would have these things at any price, and, of course, had their way to the exclusion of the vast majority who were not sufficiently well off to compete with them. And this fashion was the parent, not of another fashion, but of a craze, which raged for two years or more.

The years 1893 and 1894 I take to be those in which people, despairing of obtaining their heart's desire, turned their attention to what were known as 'Limited Editions,' and raged furiously. Nothing but a thorough grasp of the state of the book-market at the time, and a deep insight into human nature, could have hit upon the 'Limited Edition' as a stop-gap, and those who invented it are entitled to every credit for their enterprise. The apology for the life of the 'Limited Edition' brought to its logical conclusion was this: Times have changed, and, moreover, more people buy books than formerly, whether to read or to store. With the readers we have nothing to do, except incidentally; but so far as the collectors are concerned, it is obvious that only about one out of every ten can afford to pay the extremely high prices demanded for most of the first editions of the authors of repute which they affect.

Now comes the point, and upon this the whole argument succeeds or fails. Do they want these coveted books to read or to accumulate? If they wish to read them they can do so at any time, for there are more editions than one in the majority of instances, and the demand for the later and cheaper ones is of a different character altogether; *ergo*, they really want them, though they would perhaps be highly indignant if we said so, to possess and not necessarily to read. Let us, therefore, make new books in the image of the old, decorating them artistically, and printing them in the best possible style. Let us cut down the edition to a very small number of copies, in order to keep it out of the hands of all but just enough buyers to make the venture pay well, and we ought to succeed in establishing a furore that will continue precisely as long as the strenuous efforts to obtain time-tried poems and essays remain futile by reason of their cost.

The venture was purposely confined to poems and essays, because literary wares of this kind good enough for the purpose could be bought for next to nothing. A novel, in order to compete on this particular ground with the older works of Ainsworth, Thackeray, and the rest, would be costly to buy in manuscript, and difficult as well as expensive to produce; and, moreover, novels

How Fashion Lives

never pay unless they are sold in large quantities. This argument was sound throughout, and, moreover, a fresh departure of some kind was inevitable, if only to stem the tide that flowed so aggressively in favour of the rich. The venture succeeded, for almost on the instant the collector, casting a lingering look behind on the expensive works for which he craved, turned away from them, and welcomed the 'dainty volumes of delicious verse' which came tumbling down in almost endless variety. There was a scramble for them which continued exactly as long as had been predicted, namely, until the prices of once coveted books began to fall, and then the 'Limited Editions' fell too, and the craze was over, for the present at least.

One would have thought that the direct result of this procedure would have been a fresh rush to former fields, but the fact is otherwise. Original editions of the works of older poets and essayists of the highest repute are still as costly as ever, but the general ruck have fallen in the market, and remain fallen to this present day. More than that, the 'Limited Edition' brought within reasonable access innumerable better books, now become cheaper, provided they are not in the very finest condition.

Just at the moment there is no great 'boom' observable in the English market, no great craze for books of a certain special kind, though some, as usual, are sought for unceasingly, as, for example, many of those older works of English literature which were seen in such profusion in the collection of Mr. Charles B. Foote, dispersed in New York at the beginning of 1895.

Whatever hard things may be said of collectors, however much they may be likened to literary jackdaws, or to what extent their tastes may be criticised and compared with those of other people, they have a virtue—and a great one—one undisputed virtue, which, like charity, covereth a multitude of sins. This cardinal virtue is, that now, as in past times, their primary aim is to appraise literature at its true worth, and to make that the *raison d'être* of their enterprise. The inevitable red herring may lead them, for the moment, away from the pleasant places they have made their home, but it has never yet prevented their return.

And this home is among time-tried and intrinsically valuable books, and not among those which are temporarily in vogue. It is a home which existed in Greece, and in Rome, and all through the so-called Dark Ages, during the Renaissance, and down the centuries which succeeded, right to this present year of grace—a home furnished with genius and perfumed with sentiment. Look there at Paul Lacroix snatching from a Paris stall the very copy of 'Le Tartuffe' which had belonged to King Louis XIV., and later on sheltering not merely the great Pixérécourt, founder of the Société des Bibliophiles Français,

How Fashion Lives 123

but his whole library as well, until such time as his creditors had drawn off their legions and departed. Sentiment, as well as a passion for literature, was at the bottom of these acts, for that very copy of 'Le Tartuffe' had been in Molière's coat-pocket, and Pixérécourt had a tale to tell of every scholarly volume he possessed. You cannot manufacture genuine sentiment, nor is the quality to be evolved from anything except genius.

Accordingly, we find that every book which excites the cupidity of the true bibliophile derives its magic power primarily from within, and that this power is often materially increased by reason of extraneous considerations. The instances in which external matters have at any time been capable of investing an inferior book with a halo of importance or romance are so extremely rare that they might almost be counted on the fingers. A mere fleeting craze cannot do it, and it is the greatest mistake in the world to suppose that a scarce book would be sought for, and prized when found, merely because it is scarce, and for no other reason. As every book-collector is aware, there are hundreds and thousands of volumes lying neglected on the book-stalls to-day which would never be there if this were not so. Some are scarce in the sense of being difficult to meet with when wanted, but, if that be their only merit, it has never yet been acknowledged.

But fashion, though it can never make a bad

book good, has the power to subordinate one good book to another, notwithstanding, and to play shuttlecock with the names of authors and printers alike. It was fashion in excelsis which lived with the Elzevirs when men were saying to one another, 'I have all the poets they ever printed. I have ten examples of every volume, and all have red letters, and are of the right date.' It was fashion, too, which assessed the value of Longpierre's copy of Montaigne's 'Essais' (1659), with the buffalo's head on the preface and at the commencement of each chapter, at 5,100 francs, and only the other day (March 20, 1896) flung away a fine tall copy, bound by Bozerian, for the paltry sum of £6 15s.

The same capricious mistress assessed Sir Walter Raleigh's 'Discoverie of the Large, Rich and Bewtiful Empyre of Guiana,' 1626, at a comparatively low rate—£3 3s., if the late Mr. Henry Stevens is to be believed, and no one had a greater knowledge of such books than he—in 1858, notwithstanding the fact that it must be credited to Shakespeare's library, as the 'still vex'd Bermoothes,' and his knowledge of the breaking of the sea on the rugged rocks by which the Bermuda Islands are surrounded, sufficiently demonstrate. Thirty years ago Smith's 'Generall Historie of Virginia,' published for M. Sparkes in 1625, could have been got for a twentieth part of the sum that would be asked for it now, and this too is by Fashion's decree.

But in these and any number of typical instances there is no change in the estimation in which good literature is held; no lifting a book from an abyss of mediocrity and placing it on a pinnacle of fame. Fashion may swing men's minds to this or to that, and so indirectly and for the time being cause those ups and downs in the book-market which are the despair of everyone who has endeavoured to account for them, but further than this she cannot go.

And therefore, when I said that book-men are swayed by fashion, I meant that their tastes and inclinations are capricious, and not that they would, even if they could, enter upon the task of passing judgment upon the verdict of the world. Fashion may and does make rules which cannot be broken with impunity, so far as the pocket is concerned; it may even create an extraordinary and exceptional interest in one author to-day, and abandon him to-morrow, and do many other wonderful things to cause our unsympathetic neighbours to blaspheme; but the romance of book-collecting would be no romance were it stolidly kept at one dead level of insensibility. To employ a homely illustration — though Fashion may decorate a house, it can neither build one nor raze one to the ground.

CHAPTER VIII.

THE RULES OF THE CHASE.

THERE was a time, and that not so very many years ago, when old books were, if only you got out of the central mart, difficult to procure, and by no means easy to store. They were frequently in folio, huge ponderous works which, unless they were of the very best, challenged the courage of all but veterans, as they looked down from their dark corners. There was no escaping them, no getting away from their costly presence, and no reading them either without sitting at a table ; for 'literary machines' were not then invented, and no one seemed to care about lingering with arched back over a fire, with sixty or eighty pounds weight of paper on his knees. Such a discipline would have been valuable, no doubt, but learning grew lazy when it left the monasteries, and a table became a virtual necessity for most folk. After a time folios were turned into octavos, and the price cheapened. The 'extraneous Tegg,' as Carlyle calls the well-known bookseller, and our friends Cooke, Walker,

Bell, and many more, commenced to cut the throat of the trade, and to ruin the honest author, by printing favourite books at such a very cheap rate that the public soon became totally demoralized. Cooke made an enormous fortune—for a bookseller—and died amid the plaudits of the mob and the curses of his competitors, for he had out-Heroded Herod in prostituting 'Tom Jones,' a thing deemed impossible, by publishing the text in numbers, *verbatim et literatim*, at a scandalously cheap price. Then he approached other 'British novelists' in turn, and went through the entire pantheon, winding up with a series of sacred classics. Cooke was a man of immense resource, and no scruples; he got the author out of the way (I don't *say* he murdered him), sold up his rivals, and positively lived to an advanced age—three crimes which procured him hosts of enemies, but nevertheless altered the whole system of publishing, and solved for ever the problem whether it is better or worse for the producer to sell fifty articles at a penny each, or a single one of the same kind for four and two.

Now, Cooke's procedure, and that of the other booksellers who were wise enough to follow his lead, not only had great influence in moulding the character of the bibliophiles of that day, but is directly responsible even now for many of those rules and regulations which their descendants are sticklers in the preservation of. A folio had always been bound in a manner suitable to its bulk, and in such a way as to render a new binding unnecessary for a very long time, and there was, consequently, little or no necessity for rules of any kind for its preservation. When the folio was hoisted to its place, there it would stop, or, if taken down, it would be with a considerable amount of caution.

Not so Cooke's cheap and easily handled productions. They were light and airy, and bound in millboard, which, after a moderate use, never failed to come to pieces. As a matter of fact, nearly all Cooke's books met with on the stalls to-day show unmistakable evidence of honest handling. They are thumbed, perhaps torn, and always very feeble in the cover. Should it have been worth anyone's while to rebind one of these cheap little volumes, we may be sure that it will show a stout leather cover, and be scrupulously cut down to the headlines for the sake of the shavings. This cropping of margins was no crime then, because there was no rule to the contrary, and Cooke turned out his books in such numbers that they were really of very trifling value at any time. Before his day, it was a common practice for the publishers themselves to have their books bound in leather, and for the binders to cut as much of the margins away as they decently could.

For instance, let us revert to 'Tom Jones,' one of the first books experimented upon by the first of really cheap publishers. When this

The Rules of the Chase

novel came out, in 1749, it made its appearance in six small volumes bound uniformly in leather, with edges more or less cropped. This cropping process seems to have pleased Fielding immensely, or at any rate there is no doubt in the world that he preferred to see his handiwork issued in the way common to folios, rather than in boards with ragged edges, for a sample set of volumes was done up in the latter style and rejected.

We think him foolish, because not very long ago the sample set was discovered in an old farmhouse, and, after changing hands once or twice, packed off to the auction-rooms, where it realized the handsome sum of £69. A little bit of paper made an immense difference in this case, for its presence was in conformity with an imperative rule that has grown up since Fielding's day, and which lays it down that never—no, never—must a book be denuded of its margins if you wish to make the most of it. Whatever its quality, do not deprive it of the minutest fraction of its legitimate area of paper. Of course, this drastic regulation came into force when books began to be generally published, not in folio or quarto, but in a smaller and more handy size.

Collectors, whether of books or anything else, are content at first with a little. Their requirements are indeed boundless, so far as number is concerned; but they have not yet become solicitous of technical or minute distinctions. A book is a book, and a coin is a coin, and they are satisfied without it, provided it is substantially the same as some other copy of the same edition, or some other coin struck from the same die, which they happen to have. After a while, however, a very natural desire to excel produces its inevitable result, and all sorts of arbitrary variations are catalogued and insisted upon by those who have plenty of money, and at the same time pride themselves on their discrimination and taste. Thus it is that a comparatively scarce book, this first edition of 'Tom Jones,' for instance, may become excessively scarce under exceptional circumstances. True, the collector who is a terrible stickler for detail may, and probably will, be charged sooner or later with being a fool for his pains; but that penalty he is content to accept, happy in the consciousness that, when everything is said and done, he has chosen the better part, which in all these cases consists in leaving well alone.

Not long ago a London newspaper, which ought to have known better, was very angry with a collector of the circumspect school because he had boasted that all the books in his library were 'uncut.' 'This shows,' said the sage who wrote the article, 'that he has a hundred or more books which he has never read, and, what is worse has no intention of reading.' He thought that 'uncut' meant 'not cut open,' and perhaps thinks so still, for it was worth no one's while

The Rules of the Chase

to teach him his business, and so the matter dropped.

The cropping of books has, indeed, become as iniquitous as the old Star Chamber practice of cropping of ears, or perhaps even more so, for some at least of the delinquents who appeared to the usual Writ of Rebellion, which it was the practice of that tribunal to issue from time to time, richly deserved all they got. The proper way to deal with a book is to burn it if it be wicked, and if not, to leave it alone; though, if this fact had always been recognised, there would have been no scope for us in the matter of broad expanse of margin, since what everybody has no one craves for.

Fine bindings are a law unto themselves, and require separate consideration; but there is a matter connected with bindings generally, or, rather, with the advisability of binding at all, which has created a considerable amount of scandal in times past. Let us take that scarce book, 'The English Dance of Death,' which William Combe wrote in the safe seclusion of the King's Bench Prison. It appeared originally in 1815 in parts, each with its wrapper, and afterwards was bound up in two volumes, whereupon it at once lost, according to present-day ideas on the subject, five-sixths of its value.

The 'Tale of Two Cities' when in the original eight parts is worth three times as much, at least, as when in the publisher's cloth binding, and nearly all Thackeray's more important works are subject to a very considerable reduction under identical circumstances. Curiously enough, the rule is imperative in certain specific instances, while in others it has no application at all. The question whether to apply it or not depends on the character of the book. We should insist upon the parts being left unbound in the case of 'Bells and Pomegranates,' but not in that of Trusler's 1833 edition of 'Hogarth Moralized,' for here the twenty-six parts are a positive nuisance unless they are bound. Trusler's melancholy production is not much good, bound or unbound, but it will serve as an illustration, and certain it is that the cost of binding will have to be taken into consideration when estimating the worth of the numbers, in case anyone thrusts them upon a long-suffering purchaser, and will not be denied.

'Fools you are!' says Sir Ensor Doone, under other circumstances, and 'Idiots!' adds the man in the street when he reads that somebody has paid a large sum for 'Ask Mamma' in the 'original thirteen parts,' when he could, had he been so minded, have got the entire book, nicely bound, for a fourth of the money—plates, text, and all. This is the cry whenever a sum which appears exorbitant on the face of it is paid for anything.

A short time ago £445 was obtained for a fiddle by Stradivari; £798 for an imperfect silver cup made by Jacob Frölich, master of Nuremberg

The Rules of the Chase 133

in 1555; and £246 odd for a rose-point flounce of Venetian lace three yards long. Nothing was said about the enormity of these sums, but let a fiftieth·part of the smallest amount be realized at any time for a book 'in parts,' and there is a chorus of disapprobation, for which, however, it must be confessed, there is just a modicum of warrant.

It is really not at all easy to see why a series of numbers, liable at any moment to injury, and always inconvenient to handle, should, the quality of the plates, if there are any, and other accessories being equal, be so greatly preferred to a volume bound in a proper manner. Perhaps it is a matter of sentiment, perhaps of pure scarcity, or perhaps the *bonâ-fide* book-collector likes to give himself as much trouble as he possibly can, by way of purifying his life and chastening his soul. However this may be, there is no question that some books are thought more highly of when in sections, and that the public in their blindness fail to see the reason why.

Well, there is, at any rate, much less reason, one would think, in paying £246 for a lace flounce wherewith to minister to the vanity of some middle-aged dame than there is for incurring a fractional obligation for classic works, which will outlast us by many a day, even though they may have the fortune to be uncut and in parts as issued. And besides, O shade of Mr. Burgess! did you not ignore in your lifetime the rule that it were best to let well alone, and were not the consequences terrible in the extreme?*

Whether any regulations are really necessary for the proper preservation of books old or new let the bibliophiles determine; but so long as they exist it is folly to ignore them. Nay, further, to be as far upon the safe side as possible, we must prefer to buy our books with due regard to those rules and orders which our progenitors have in their wisdom drawn up, selecting the very best copies we can afford to pay or obtain credit for, and even going to the length of investing in 'parts' which shall not shame us, or cause us loss when the inevitable hour of parting arrives.

The cardinal rule of the game is triple-headed, and it is this: Buy the best you can, spend what you find convenient without stint, and, above all, keep to the track you have mapped out for yourself and have so far followed. Then will it be well with you now and hereafter in all things bookish. Act the contrary throughout, and every stiver you spend will swell the total of your confusion; drop by drop the clepsydra of your fortunes will run out to your bane.

* The library of the late Mr. Frederick Burgess was sold by Messrs. Sotheby on May 31 and three subsequent days, 1894. It consisted almost entirely of then 'Fashionable' books, illustrated by Cruikshank and other talented artists. Parts had been bound up, original cloth covers removed, and expensive bindings substituted, not merely in a few instances, but as a general rule. The collection, though an excellent one of its kind, was disposed of at an enormous sacrifice.

But the rules which hem in the book-buyer, and direct his course, are not solely confined to technical points and details such as those mentioned. On the contrary, they are equally stringent in many other respects, and in particular as to the description of book to buy, its condition, and so on; for it is taken for granted that no man, or at least no bookman worthy the name, would purchase a bad or inferior edition when he could get a better, or a volume that was imperfect or had been shamefully used by a succession of careless owners. Between the quality of one edition and another there is often an immense difference, as all the world knows, or ought to know. That edition of '"Paradise Lost," a Poem in twelve books, the author John Milton, Printed for the Proprietors and sold by all the Booksellers,' no date, but about 1780, is one of the very worst that any misguided man ever picked up from a street stall. The mistakes, not merely in punctuation, but in spelling, are too gross and scandalous for mention; entire lines are not infrequently missing, and whole sentences often perverted. Contrast this with any copy of the first edition, no matter which title-page may have heralded it into the world, and we have a different book entirely. The rule says that, though an ordinary copy of the first edition may be three thousand times as valuable in money as this gutter abortion, you must nevertheless not be attracted by the latter because it is cheap—no, not even though you should think it good enough for everyday use.

Naturally enough there are free-lances among bookmen, people who are a law unto themselves, and insist upon doing precisely as they like, but it will be noticed that they very rarely fly in the face of any rule in important cases. Your free-lance has the courage of the Seven Champions of Christendom when face to face with Stackhouse's 'History of the Bible,' but let him, for example, come across 'Tamerlaine, and other Poems, By a Bostonian;' not Herne Shepherd's London reprint, but the original tract which Calvin F. S. Thomas printed at Boston in 1827. Let us suppose also that it is in its original tea-tinted paper covers, just as Edgar Allen Poe sent it forth into the world. What would our free-lance do? Have it rebound in defiance of the rule? Hardly, for if he did he would reduce the importance of his exceptionally fortunate find, and therefore its value, to such a considerable extent that even he would hesitate long before committing himself to an act that could never be recalled. Moreover, he would have direct evidence with regard to a copy of this very pamphlet before his eyes, for a collector once really did pick one up for a few pence. In the first place, let it be stated that only three copies of 'Tamerlaine' can now be traced. One is in the British Museum, which acquired it from the late Mr. Henry Stevens for one shilling. A second was found on a stall in America for the equivalent of something less, and it is this latter copy which furnishes the evidence referred to. The fortunate finder sent it to Messrs. C. F. Libbie and Co., the auctioneers of Boston, who sold it by auction in 1893 for the equivalent of £370 to the agents of Mr. George F. Maxwell, of New York, who had the pamphlet rebound in magnificent style by Lortic Fils, at a cost of several hundred dollars. Moreover, the covers were bound in, and the edges left untrimmed. No expense was spared; everything was done in proper order according to rule of thumb. Yet in April, 1895, when Mr. Maxwell's valuable library was sold by the same auctioneers, this copy of 'Tamerlaine,' vastly improved as one might think, dropped to £290, showing a clear loss of £80, irrespective altogether of the amount paid for binding, auctioneers' commission, and so on.

It may, of course, be said that it is a common thing for the same book to bring different amounts at different times, even when the sales take place within a few months of each other. A bookseller, dissatisfied with the amount bid for some scarce work he has put on the market, will frequently buy it in and offer it again later on with satisfactory results.

But 'Tamerlaine' is an altogether exceptional piece, and, moreover, where were the gentlemen who respectively bid £360 and £365 on the occasion when Mr. Maxwell secured it for a slightly larger sum ? Wherever they were, they seem to have been fully alive to the fact that 'Tamerlaine' was not as it was when Poe sent it out for review ever so many years ago. 'Ah, broken is the golden bowl,' and it is to be feared by that talented binder, Lortic Fils. If ever I find 'Tamerlaine,' I shall keep every binder at arm's length, and not be tempted to paint the lily—no, not even though Derome himself should rise from the dead and offer to array it gratuitously in morocco, tooled to a heavenly pattern, and powdered all over with the fleurs-de-lys of imperial France. In this spirit let us reproduce the title-page of 'Tamerlaine,' as a Frontispiece to this Romance, so that we shall know it on the instant if the gods should only guide our feet to where a fourth copy lies hidden away. Then let us remember the rule to let well alone, and be thankful, for it is a rule of gold, the first and foremost of them all.

Never to outrage sentiment, always to identify one's self with the author as far as possible, is to respect both the living and the dead, and to make life comparatively easy, even though its path be strewn with flints and cobble-stones. May the person who has the maximum of respect for the private life and character of one of the greatest of modern poets eventually acquire the shabby copy of 'The Eve of St. Agnes' which the luckless half-immortal thrust into his pocket as the *Don Juan* was sent to the bottom of the Gulf

The Rules of the Chase

of Genoa. It will come with a train of associations that will on the instant forbid the elimination of a single stain, or the slightest repair of its sea-swept cover.

The book-hunter who has the feelings and aspirations of an ancient race properly diffused through his system would almost give his head for a relic such as this, for his passion is not to be stifled. He likes to think that the books he reads and handles have a pedigree, that they come to him laden with the fears and aspirations of the past, that they are ghost-haunted, and that they who wrote them, though dead, yet speak, not as man to man, but as soul to soul.

CHAPTER IX.

THE GLAMOUR OF BINDINGS.

THERE being in very truth no new thing under the sun, it would be egotistical in the highest degree, and absurd, to assert positively that the argument about to be advanced is at all novel, though it may certainly appear strange. It is, however, original so far as I am concerned, for I have not seen it hinted at before by anyone, much less carried to a conclusion. Whether there be any warrant for it or no is a point for others, who have a greater capacity for distinguishing reason in probabilities than I can lay claim to, to determine for themselves.

It is admitted by all writers who have studied the subject of bookbinding from its historical aspect, that, as the monks of the Middle Ages were the sole producers of books, so also they were the only binders, and that the record of their achievements dates from about 520 A.D., when Dagæus, the Irish monk, practised his art, to the invention of printing from movable types by Gutenberg and Füst nearly a thousand years later.

The Glamour of Bindings 141

Not merely in England, but all over Europe, the monks were practically the sole custodians of knowledge during the earlier part of this period; they alone produced books, they alone bound them, they alone could read them. There were, no doubt, laymen who could read and write, but neither accomplishment was general in the outer world. King Alfred (A.D. 870) was a scholar; William the Conqueror, two centuries later, could neither read nor write.

The Stowe MS. No. 960 contains all that remains of the register of Hyde Abbey, Winchester, from the time of King Canute, one of its earliest benefactors, to the Dissolution. Among the many interesting articles in this Stowe manuscript there is one which exceeds all the rest in interest, for it bears the actual cross, sign or signature made by William in testimony that he had granted 9 hides of land to the monks, in exchange for the site of the cemetery in the city of Winchester. The King has drawn with a quill a rude and most illiterate cross, if such a thing can be imagined. The ink has not flown evenly from a pen evidently held in a perpendicular position with tremulous and infirm grip. Each line begins with a splutter, and at the point of intersection there is what looks suspiciously like a blot. It is obvious at the first glance that King William, though a man of many accomplishments eminently useful in those days, was accustomed to wield the battle-axe rather than the pen. And this was so general for centuries after his day that, but for the monks, there would have been no learning at all, and no books all that time.

It is unnecessary to refer to this phase of the matter further than to say that all the ancient and medieval European manuscripts which still exist were written by ecclesiastics, and doubtless bound by them as well. Manuscripts of the ninth century, beautifully encased in ivory, silver and gold, and sometimes encrusted with precious stones, are still extant. These are undoubtedly monkish, and the question arises, What has become of the vast bulk of which these are but a remnant? What has become of the old English libraries that existed in hundreds at the time of the Reformation? Were they, all but a very few, wantonly destroyed by those who undertook the spoliation of the monasteries, or did many escape them? and if so, where are they now? The suggestion that innumerable volumes, particularly those which were handsomely and expensively bound, would never be seen by the raiders at all is not so improbable as it may at first sight appear, when we come to consider the facts.

In November, 1534, an Act of Parliament declared that 'the King's Highness was the supreme head of the Church of England, and had authority to reform and redress all errors, heresies, and abuses in the same.' This Act was speedily followed up, for in 1535 Cromwell, in his capacity of Vicar-General, proceeded to make a visitation

The Glamour of Bindings 143

of the monasteries, where he is said to have found such evidences of shameless immorality that another Act was passed, transferring such of these establishments to the Crown as were not of the annual value of £200.

The number of religious houses at this time dissolved, raided and sacked amounted to 376. With diabolical minuteness the revenues of each and all were estimated to the last penny. Bangor was worth £151 3s., and was accordingly seized on the spot. St. David easily escaped for the time being, for the revenue of that monastery proved to be £426 2s. 1d. St. Asaph, being assessed at £202 10s., escaped an early wreck by £2 10s. It was the same all over England and Wales. The revenue was estimated, and if it fell below £200, the monastery was at once filled with armed men, while Cromwell's experts stripped the walls of their arras, seized the gold and silver vessels, tore up the books, scoured the neighbourhood round about for game, tapped the vintage, and thoroughly enjoyed themselves in their own peculiar way.

It is recorded that priceless books and manuscripts were wantonly destroyed, tombs sacrilegiously broken to pieces for the sake of the metal, often merely lead or brass, that extolled the virtues or the lineage of those who slept below; silver and gold plate of exquisite workmanship, and of a degree of antiquity rarely, if ever, seen now, were melted down and sold by weight; buildings of an architectural beauty unsurpassed anywhere were wantonly defaced, and in many cases dismantled, for the sake of the materials, and in the midst of this disgraceful scene of plunder and desecration, the destroyers fought with one another as desperately as Roman gladiators of the days of Nero, for the possession of some coveted jewel or ornament that all wanted and only one could have.

Now here comes the crux of the argument. Only the smaller houses were dissolved at this time, and unless human nature were totally different in the days of Henry VIII. from what it is now, unless the Abbots of Furness, Bolton, Fountains, and other large and extremely rich monasteries, looked on unmoved while their humbler brethren were stripped to the skin and flung destitute into the lanes and ditches to die, then it is morally certain that they would take steps to protect themselves, as far as lay in their power, from the fury of the storm which they must have known would shortly burst over their heads. Unless they were wholly infatuated, they would cautiously and gradually remove their choicest possessions, their basins, images, censers, crucifixes and chalices, and above all their precious volumes, with which the very history and fortunes of the abbey were associated, and *bury them* deep down, perhaps fifteen or twenty feet, under the walls.

The ruin brought at this time upon all that was

priceless by reason of its antiquity and associations is incalculable, and the only ray of consolation let in upon these dark days' doings is that the Abbots of the larger monasteries, taking warning from what they saw going on all around, may have buried their choicest possessions, where, perhaps, they will be found some of these days, when the plough shall furrow up the dust of Furness or Denever.

Many of the inventories taken by the King's agents are extant. One of them, that of Fountains, taken just before the Dissolution, will suffice to show what is meant. The value of all the plate, gold and silver, amounted to £708 5s. 9¾d.—a comparatively small sum, seeing that the cattle, sheep and swine belonging to the abbey were of much greater value. Not a single book of any kind is scheduled, and yet the library of Fountains was at one time the most extensive and important in Yorkshire. As the Knights Templars buried their gold under the high altar in the church of the New Temple, yet standing within sound of the roar of Fleet Street, in order to protect it against the rapacity of Edward I., so it is suggested that the Abbots of Fountains and other surviving houses buried their treasures in the most sacred place they could think of, thereby handing them over, as it were, to God and the right, rather than abandon them to the tender mercies of man.

Now, this is merely an argument based upon

probability; it cannot, from the very nature of
the case, be supported by a scrap of evidence, and
yet it carries with it such a ring of truth in my
ears that, were I the happy owner of one of those
fast-crumbling piles which still rear their rugged
fronts to the sky, I would, by all the enamels of
Limoges, by the ivory, gold and silver, and rubies
which make up this glamour of bindings unseen,
put the argument to the test without hesitation
and regardless of cost.

Monastic bindings of English workmanship
are not, as we may well understand, distinguished
as a rule for extreme beauty. The gorgeous
covers that protected illuminated manuscripts,
themselves extremely valuable, were in vogue at a
very early period, long before the invention of
printing, and the vast majority were probably
either hidden away as suggested, or destroyed.
In any case, however, they must have been rare
even a thousand years ago—as rare, indeed, as
the exceptionally fine missals and breviaries they
protected, some of which would take a monk his
lifetime to produce. We find that by the four-
teenth century monastic bindings were usually
serviceable and plain, and that it was only occasionally that rich materials were employed, as,
for example, when a King's library was added
to, or some important monastery gave a special
order by way of continuing the traditions of the
house, and showing that time had not in any
way curtailed its glories. The most interesting

The Glamour of Bindings 147

ancient bindings that yet survive to us consist of a specimen of the work of the monk Dagæus, which dates from about 520 A.D., and a manuscript known as the 'Textus Sanctus Cuthberti,' bound in velvet with a broad silver border, and inlaid with gems, by the first English binder, one Bilfred, a monk of Durham, who was living at the beginning of the eighth century. This is the holy volume that was swallowed up by the sea, and, according to the old legend, restored out of respect for the memory of the saint, or perhaps that of the monk or both.

We have, therefore, two styles of monastic bindings—one resplendent in gold, ivory, and precious stones, and the other of a more sober character for ordinary and daily use. The latter were of wood covered with embossed leather, or with plain shark skin, or even seal. They were ponderous, massive folios of great weight and durability, protected in vulnerable parts with brass or iron bosses and corner-plates. We find them produced as a matter of course to about the time of the Renaissance, when they gradually gave place to smaller books bound in velvet or silk, and embroidered by abbesses and nuns, and so the custom prevailed until the days of the first printers, when calf and morocco were introduced from the East by the Venetians, and pigskin or thick parchment became fashionable. Prior to this time oaken boards formed the groundwork of every binding, and to this day the word 'boards' is in general use, although the reason for its existence obtains no longer.

The Italians were the first to awaken to a sense of the propriety of things, and the modern collector to whom bindings appeal with an irresistible force instinctively turns to the first Italian era to supply him with some of the rarest and choicest examples of the art. The commoner monastic bindings have no beauty in his eyes, and those of a superior order and more costly finish are practically interred within the walls of great public institutions, from which they will, in the nature of things, never emerge. For some reason or other the finest binding loses its glamour, if not its interest, when exhibited in a glass case. We must have these things for our own before we can appreciate them to the full. What more melancholy mortal than a public curator trying to work himself up into a state of enthusiasm as he describes the objects committed to his care? They are mere pots and pans and 'things,' but yet how different if he had them all at home!

But to return to our bindings. Let it be observed that with the invention of printing, and the consequent production of books in a more portable form, the modern style of binding was gradually introduced. These were the days of deep-toned leathers, ornamented in gold and variegated colours, and executed for wealthy and powerful Italian families, who employed skilful artists to draw the designs, often consisting of

The Glamour of Bindings 149

geometrical interlacings or foliage, such as Maioli and Grolier rejoiced in.

This style of ornamenting leather came from the East, as did the Saracenic rope ornament, which was perhaps the first design to take the fancy of Italian workmen. The general appearance of this rope design reminds one of the frontispiece to a certain 'Biography of Jack Ketch,' which someone brought out a few years ago. The half-length portrait of the hero is within a graceful border of ropes intertwined, there are ropes tumbling from the clouds, and he holds a rope in his hand, as if ready to begin. Behind, so far as my memory serves me, there is the frowning portal of Newgate, festooned with fetters. A panel of Saracenic rope-design set on end reminds one of this frontispiece, and we listen instinctively for the tolling of the prison bell.

The celebrated printer Aldus Manutius seems to have been the first to rebel against such sinister designs as these, and, moreover, he was the friend of Jean Grolier and Thommaso Maioli, princes among book-lovers, and artists by nature. Aldus often bound the books he printed in smooth, rich morocco, tooled in gold to various patterns of elaborate design, and to him we doubtless owe much of the improvement in binding which became so marked at the beginning of the sixteenth century. His were, indeed, publishers' bindings produced by rule of thumb, but they are not on that account less worthy of interest, for the name of Aldus is one to conjure with in all things bookish.

The Thommaso Maioli to whom reference has been made exercised a much greater influence than Aldus ever did in the matter of bindings, for his were the models on which were fashioned the designs of later collectors, not merely of Italy, but of France and other European countries. Maioli's designs are free and open, in a style suggestive of Eastern influence, but reduced to earth and reality by perpendicular and perfectly straight lines. His library was open to his friends, and most of his books were lettered on the covers 'Tho. Maioli et amicorum,' qualified sometimes by other words of different import, ' Ingratis servire nephas.' Very likely Maioli was on occasion the victim of some too ardent bibliophile, who would think nothing of borrowing, and perhaps also of some Philistine, who left ruin in the trail of his dirty or heavy fingers.

So, too, Jean Grolier, whom Dibdin ludicrously turns into a bookbinder, but who was, in fact, the French contemporary and twin soul of Maioli, chose to follow the traditions of all true booklovers, and his covers also bear the courteous invitation to friends, ' Io Grolierii et amicorum,' though he too found occasion to alter it from time to time.

The bindings of Maioli and Grolier, worked out and finished most probably at Venice for the most part, are highly valued by collectors all over the

The Glamour of Bindings 151

world, and they are indeed worthy of all the attention they receive.

The bindings of Maioli are more difficult to meet with than those of Grolier, because the library of the latter numbered some 8,000 volumes, and was eventually sold by auction and dispersed broadcast. Grolier's descendants had no false sentiment in their composition; the 'amici' were themselves, and they acted in their own interests, in strict accordance with their interpretation of the family motto. Besides, in those days, though the love of books raged furiously in isolated breasts, in general it was cold, and no one could probably have been found to take over the entire library, or even that considerable portion of it which at the last lay among the dust and cobwebs of the Hôtel de Vic.

Rarer than any of this period, however, are the medallion bindings of Demetrio Canevari, physician to Pope Urban VII., who was living in the year 1600. In all probability Canevari merely inherited his books, for their covers belong to an earlier period. Still, whatever the fact in this respect, they are called after his name, and are very scarce, notwithstanding that the whole library was intact at Genoa until 1823. Libri thought that these delicate and elaborate bindings had never been surpassed, and certainly they are very beautiful, with their cameos in gold, silver, and colours enriched with classical portraits and mythological scenes.

But to the lover of bindings it is Grolier, Grolier, Grolier; from the haunting music of that name there is no escape, and, moreover, Grolier even in death was great. The Emperor Charles V. did not disdain to follow his taste, while Francis I. was completely carried away by it, his bindings, as soon as he could shake off the early influence of Étienne Roffet, being magnificently Grolier-esque, blazing with gold and the brightest colours. Then came Henri II. and the accomplished Diane de Poictiers, whose emblems, the crescent moon, the bow, quiver and arrows of the chase, are invariably found associated with the initial of the King. Diane was the royal mistress, and seems to have had a passion for blending the two linked D's with the regal H. This joint monogram was on the walls and furniture of her Château of Anet, and still stares us out of countenance occasionally from behind glass doors. Diane, however, so long as she had it in her power—that is to say, until 1559, when the King died—did everything she could to introduce a taste for magnificent and sumptuous bindings into France; to eclipse once and for all time the efforts of every book-lover who had preceded her. In a measure she succeeded, and certainly no good books come to us, when they come at all, which is but seldom, breathing more of romance than these volumes which Diane treasured till her dying day, in spite of Court frowns and persecution. Her library, which was a very extensive

The Glamour of Bindings 153

one, remained intact at Anet until 1723, when it was sold.

It would be almost an endless task to name all the patrons of artistic bindings who lived in France up to about the time of the Revolution. There was the legitimate Queen of Henri II., Catherine de Medicis, a descendant of the great Lorenzo, called the Magnificent, whose books are often covered in white calf, powdered with golden flowers. This lady was an enthusiastic booklover, who, when she died, left a library of some 4,000 volumes, most of which are still to be seen in the Bibliothèque Nationale.

Then we must not forget her son, Francis II., who married the unfortunate Mary, Queen of Scots. His bindings, whether stamped with the golden dolphin or with a monogram in which his own and the Queen's initials are interlaced, are extremely scarce, and worth much gold. Francis was only seventeen when he died, and had, consequently, no time to become thoroughly saturated with the intense longing for beautiful decorations which probably did much to set Catherine de Medicis and the fair Diane by the ears. His younger brother, afterwards Henri III., had greater opportunities for indulging his tastes in this respect, and the history of his bibliopegic life, so to speak, is full of strange surprises.

Like all other bindings with a history, specimens from the library of this gloomy and taciturn monarch are very rarely met with. They are distinctly worth looking at, however, especially by those of a morbid turn of mind. They are more suggestive than the Saracenic rope style, and infinitely more eloquent of woe. Henri ought to have married the Princess Condé, but she died, and the young King, then about twenty-four years old, and apparently influenced by the example of his father and mother, turned for consolation to his library, and the designing of emblems congenial to his mood.

These consist, at least at this period, when his grief was young and fresh, of skulls garnished with cross-bones, tears, and other emblems of the grave. They are, in their way, absolutely unique, and much more remarkable than the curled snake of Colbert or the three towers of Madame de Pompadour. The bindings of Henri III., though uncongenial to most tastes, are of excellent design and workmanship, for Nicholas and Clovis Eve were living in his day, and better artists than they proved themselves to be it would be hopeless to look for. It was one or other of the brothers who introduced the fanfare style, which resolved itself finally into a profusion of small flourished ornaments, so closely worked together that a volume bound in this way looked as though picked out ethereally with sprays, scrolls, and showers of golden rain. The fanfare style was, so it is said, introduced to put an end to the suicidal gloom that had overtaken the Court of Henri III.

The Glamour of Bindings 155

That monarch, though a bad man, was probably the most original thinker in the matter of bindings who ever lived, for De Thou's plan of inventing a fresh design every time he got married resolved itself into nothing more than a series of heraldic changes, and De Thou is generally credited with a considerable amount of ingenuity, and regarded as a person distinctly worth collecting on account of the variations in which he is found, and for other reasons. Every book which touches, however remotely, on the subject of bindings never fails to give the armorial bearings of De Thou at different periods of his life; and we must pass on to Marguerite de Valois; not the celebrated Queen of Navarre who wrote the 'Heptameron' in her youth, but the daughter of Henri II., already mentioned as a great lover of bindings. Marguerite very appropriately, having regard to the origin of her name, chose designs of daisies, which she placed in oval compartments bearing the quarterings of Valois, the whole being surrounded with leafy and branching scroll-work. Clovis Eve was her binder, and the work he turned out at this period is in his best style.

The history of bookbinding takes a curious turn at this epoch. Hitherto we have heard more of the patron than of the artist, a state of things which from this time forth exists no longer. I would not commit myself to the assertion that Marguerite de Valois, who, by the way, died in 1615, was the last of the great collectors who eclipsed the reputation of the binders they employed; but I know that about this period we begin to hear more of the workman and less of the patron. When everybody of the least importance begins to collect books, and to have them bound in specially designed covers, the artist rises on the ashes of the amateur, whose day is from that time forth over and gone, except in the limited circle in which he moves. So it was at the epoch which immediately followed the death of Marguerite de Valois. The Eves had forced their way into notice in spite of the overwhelming presence of Henri II., Diane de Poictiers and Charles IX., Henri III. and IV., and other less-exalted persons; and now Le Gascon made his presence felt still more forcibly than they.

Le Gascon, who is identified with one Florimond Badier, introduced a style of ornamentation known as *pointillé*, consisting of graceful geometrical designs worked out with innumerable minute gold dots, usually on a ground of bright scarlet. The effect of a perfectly fresh and bright binding by Le Gascon must have been brilliant in the extreme; but, alas! the cost was something phenomenal, and the style, after being parodied and imitated by mechanical process, finally died out in France some thirty-five years after its introduction. Mazarin was the great patron of Le Gascon, and many books which once belonged to the great Cardinal are found with ornamentation, arms and motto—' His Fulta Manebunt '—laboriously picked out in the beautiful *pointillé* style.

During the latter part of the sixteenth century, and during the whole of the seventeenth, the French bookbinders had no equal, and if they afterwards deteriorated, they had still many great names among their ranks. Padeloup's binding of a ' Daphne et Chloe ' of 1718, with the arms of the Duke of Orleans, then Regent of France, is a masterpiece ; and then there are his bindings in mosaic, looking like lace-work, and the masterly designs worked out for Madame de Pompadour, Queen Maria Leczinska, and many other celebrities. Derome, the Abbé Du Sueil, and Monnier were all fine binders, whose work is eagerly sought for. And then comes the French Revolution, which for the time being seems to have utterly demoralized art in all its branches. Most modern collectors who affect notable bindings have to look to later days, when the surge and storm of the turmoil had passed away, and when Thouvenin, Bauzonnet, Duru, Trantz, Lortic, Marius-Michel, and many more, were in their prime.

English bindings, so far as past times are concerned, were never remarkable for refinement or taste. Velvet or silk, frequently embroidered and tasselled, was often used for royal books, and we also meet with pasteboard covered with leather and studded with gilt ornaments on the back.

There is, however, not a trace of the genius of Le Gascon or Derome in any of these productions, and the designs show very little originality. Occasionally, however, an English binding is produced which, bound in morocco—the introduction of which is placed to the credit of James I.—has an extremely good effect, as in the case of the 'Pontificale Romanum,' 1595, now in the British Museum. This specimen is elaborately gold-tooled with the arms and badges of the King. A facsimile of it will be found facing page 228 of Mr. W. Salt Brassington's 'History of the Art of Bookbinding.' It is a clever and characteristic piece of work in brown morocco, and gives a very good idea of the highest form of English art of the period which it was possible to produce.

The English, however, have never been at any period particularly conspicuous for their talent in the art of designing book-covers, and it is probable that the majority of well-informed persons who have not made a study of this branch of art would, in case they were asked to enumerate half a dozen good binders of English nationality, find themselves unable to mention more than one. They would begin and end with the talented but eccentric and thirsty Roger Payne, whose bindings are often original and elegant, and who might, had he been able to keep himself respectable, have attained an excellence worthy of the palmy days of France. But Payne chose to live in a tumbledown garret, denuded of plaster, and spent his money in the proportion of

For bacon ... 1 half-penny
For liquor ... 1 shilling

He was, moreover, dirty and ill-conditioned, and the only thing that saved him from utter ruin even in his youth was the painful necessity of having to work for a very long time in order to earn what any binder of the present day would look upon as a trifle. Nevertheless, Payne was, when he applied himself, a most conscientious artist, and, although the owner of some costly manuscript or volume would certainly have been horrified to find it lying in a corner of his garret, waiting its turn in company with an old shoe or two, and the remains of the food which Payne had been consuming a week or two before, yet he might be sure that he would get his treasure back in the end, not the worse for its company, but bound in a style that could not be equalled anywhere but in Paris, and not even there at the same small cost.

Some of Payne's bindings—for he had his moods—are beautiful, classical, and surprisingly artistic, and, notwithstanding his failing, it is clear that he worked hard on occasion. In fact, it is the opinion of many authorities that no English-born binder has ever succeeded, from that day to this, in approaching the genius of Payne. Walther, Staggemeier, and Kalthoeber, though they worked in London, were all Germans. Lewis may or may not have equalled his predecessor, and the same remark applies to Rivière and Bedford, whose names, however, are too contemporary to invite comparison. Besides, the question is one of individual preference, after all, and any binder, however excellent, may have to yield the palm to another in some specific matters of detail.

The glamour of a binding, indeed, vanishes when criticism steps forward. The indescribable something, which is at the same time everything, falls to pieces the instant dissecting implements are produced, and the effect is gone on the instant. The whole work of art must be regarded, and no single part of it, and we may then dream, if we like, of all the strange things that happened when it was ushered into the world. It is a pity that antique and historic bindings are so extremely difficult to procure. No one but a millionaire could hope to stock his shelves with a representative assortment of bindings of different epochs and schools, and even he might spend his whole life in searching for them.

There is something in a binding which fascinates, and yet hurls back the inspired sneer of Robbie Burns with interest:

> 'Through and through the inspired leaves,
> Ye maggots, make your windings;
> But, oh! respect his lordship's taste,
> And spare his golden bindings.'

The Glamour of Bindings

Yes! some bindings are of greater interest, from every possible point of view, than the leaves they protect, and but for their kindly care other leaves which exist among our choicest possessions might have been utterly destroyed. Many a book has been saved from death by the glamour of its cover, and will yet be saved.

CHAPTER X.

THE HAMMER AND THE END.

THE past ten years have witnessed rather more than 600 high-class sales of books by auction in London alone, and the vast majority of the collections dispersed to the winds during that period of time were not fifty, nor forty, and, at a venture, not thirty years old. Nay! it would be tolerably safe to go still further, and to say that the life of a library is, as a rule, less than half that of a man. Though it may consist of the products of antiquity, it has but a short period of existence before it as a whole; and as book is added to book, and manuscript to manuscript, and the sum total of volumes of either kind continues to increase, so, too, it is all but certain that the closing scene of its dissolution draws nearer and nearer to the end.

Generally speaking, the larger and more important a collection, the shorter its life. There are exceptions, but they only prove the rule, which may fairly be described as universal. Books are a valuable species of personal property, and next-of-kin often prove unsympathetic and unsentimental in the custody of them; besides, books cannot be divided so satisfactorily as coin, and the first and almost necessary step is to turn them into money when an estate has to be distributed among many. This is the reason why there are so few great collections in the hands of private individuals, and why they are in jeopardy every day and hour.

In this respect, then, the life of a book is even less than that of a man—an analogy which in no wise minimizes the value of existence to either. A good deal of enjoyment can be crowded into a compass of thirty years, and much information may be obtained in that period if only it be sought for aright. To ask *cui bono?* is a beggarly interrogatory which might with equal force be thrust before all life's actions, and I would not have it supposed that in my opinion it is a proper or even a satisfactory question to put where books are concerned. I only deplore the fact that to accumulate is usually to scatter the seeds of a short-lived enjoyment which dies in October. Hence it is that lovers of books have been known to cheat time and the hour, and to gratify their own inclinations as fully as possible, taking steps to secure their treasures from the hammer and the end, and have with these objects established national libraries of the very utmost importance —libraries which may certainly be destroyed in some great conflagration or by the rush of shot and shell, but can never be dispersed for the sake of the money they would produce, and will practically, therefore, remain intact for many centuries.

This, it would seem, is really the only effectual way of preserving the good and permanent things of this life for the benefit of those who come after us, for the hammer, though it never destroys directly, does so indirectly, if it be a fact that the whole is greater in every quality, save number, than the parts which compose it. Here is an instance of the contrary plan of hedging round our possessions with stipulations and directions designed for their preservation. Among the great failures of book-men let this be chronicled.

The mind travels back some five or six years to one of the high-priests of a fast-decaying cult. He lodged at a farm-house which, being in the direct path of advancing streets, has perhaps by this time been pulled down. At the time of which I speak it stood in an ocean of mud, not far from the highroad—a relic in the midst of surroundings so painfully new that few strangers who wandered that way failed to pause at the wicket-gate, and gaze on the thatched roof and warped windows that time had doomed. Once or twice a year, seldom oftener—for book-men of the type of the one who held sway there hate to be disturbed—I used to claim admission to the one moderately large room that the house possessed. Its walls were lined with books from floor to

The Hammer and the End 165

ceiling, and a number of movable cases mapped out the surface into narrow alleys. Some thousands of volumes, all bound alike, and consisting chiefly of historical works in English and Latin, must have been here stored. There were many rare books, and all were good of their kind, and most had been well read. The ways of their owner, the lifelong occupant of this crumbling cottage, were peculiar. He would get up at ten in the morning to the minute, and after breakfast take a walk in the fields, or perhaps to the city, returning at five precisely, winter and summer alike. He was so accurate in his movements that people used to set their watches by him, the new clock being generally out of gear. At half-past five he drank tea out of an enormous basin, and smoked a clay pipe, which it was his pleasure to light with a burning coal or at the chimney of his lamp. Matches he detested, on account of the sulphur, which, he said, fouled the tobacco and made it unbearable. At seven the business of the day commenced, and was continued till two, and sometimes three, in the morning—the business of reading hard without cessation, except to take a pull at the basin or to fill and light the pipe. Very pleasant were the winter evenings, when the wind howled round the gables of the house, as it often did, and the night was as black as pitch. This had gone on for thirty years without much, if any, variation, until one day the bookworm was found dead at his post, surrounded by the only real friends he had in the world, for the safety of which he had provided as follows :

By his will, made some twelve months previously, he directed that the whole of his property of every description, books excepted, should be turned into money and divided between two persons named in equal shares. The books he bequeathed to another worm, who lived a mile or two away, and who used occasionally to drop in to compare notes, subject, however, to the express condition that they should neither be sold nor otherwise parted with, and be kept in the same state in which they then were. For their further preservation he directed that the legatee should have the use of the books for his life only, and that after his death they should become the absolute property of a third person, at that time comparatively young in years, a good scholar, and a man of money. One would certainly have thought that these precautions would have sufficed to preserve this library intact for a very considerable length of time ; but, as events turned out, it was carted off within a month and sold piecemeal by auction to the highest bidders.

In the first place, it seems, the owner for life had looked over the books, and not finding them sufficiently representative of the particular branch of study to which he devoted himself, went to the reversioner and proposed a joint sale. The latter demurred, not, indeed, to the general principle, but to the suggested division of the proceeds. He said that a life interest in the hands of a man of fifty was worth less than a prospective inheritance of the whole by one much younger, and in this he was right. An actuary very quickly calculated the shares, and then came the hammer and the end.

There are hundreds and thousands of such cases, but not many bookworms of the type I have mentioned. They are fast dying out, for they belong to a very old school, which has no part or lot in these go-ahead days. It would be pitiable to hear a graybeard say farewell to a class of boys, and to see him totter to the door, which, as Epictetus says, is always open; and still more pitiable would it be if we could enter into his thoughts and regrets. Fortunately, we are as yet spared the pain of such partings as these, for our school is new—brand new—and what few old-time book-men are left feel out of place therein. Rather do they regard us in the light of merry roisterers growing wise by painful stages, whose presence is not as yet mellowed by experience, nor sanctified by the touch of time.

And so there are two schools of book-men, one closed to all but the very few, the other open to all who choose to enter, and in each there is a table laden with delights. But at the head of each alike sits the skeleton of Egyptian orgies, veiled, perhaps, after the manner of later and more effeminate times, but still there. It is the same skeleton that startled the Epicurean in the heyday of his pleasures, and threatened him ere the banquet was half over. So also it menaces us, for it clutches a hammer, and we know that it will very shortly proclaim

THE END.

Elliot Stock, 62, Paternoster Row, London.

www.ingramcontent.com/pod-product-compliance
Lightning Source LLC
Chambersburg PA
CBHW031447160426
43195CB00010BB/893